TRIVI
BOOK OF WOW

WONDERFULLY WEIRD FACTS & WHATNOT.
FOR THE SERIOUSLY CURIOUS.

Robin Why

1,369 FACTS.

Why?

An interesting feature of 1,369 is that it is a perfect square. If you take the square root of 1,369, you get 37.
37 X 37 = 1,369

And 37 is my lucky number...

For all the curious people.

Disclaimer
While the facts in this book have been verified by an independent fact-checker, it is important to note that errors and inaccuracies may still exist. Users are advised to independently verify details and use their discretion when relying on the provided information. The content is subject to change, and the publisher assumes no responsibility for any consequences resulting from the use of the information presented.

Polite Note to the Reader
This book is written in British English except where fidelity to other languages or accents are appropriate. Some words and phrases may differ from US English.

MONKEY PUZZLE...

I'm small in size but big in fun, A game of knowledge for everyone. Questions abound, answers to find, A challenge for your curious mind.

In pubs or halls, I take my place, A quiz for all, a friendly race. Facts and figures, you must know, To win the game and steal the show.

What am I, this pursuit so dear? A test of wits, so crystal clear. Gather friends, let's play the game, In this pursuit, I hold the fame.

What am I?

Check your answer on page 233!

CONTENTS

A QUICK INTRODUCTION

There are many reasons to say 'Wowwww!' Here, you'll find them all...

... from the **incredible**,

> Imagine being able to see 100 times more colours than the average person.

... to the **bewildering**,

> How can someone climb Mount Everest wearing only a pair of shorts?

... to the **really, truly silly**. (My favourite category.)

> Who convinced a nation that spaghetti grows on trees?

But ultimately, I hope you're left full to the brim with wisdom and awe, and ready to step curiously into this world of utter wonder.

Go on, get stuck in. Over 200 pages of 'Wow' await!

Yours inquisitively,
Robin Why

WONDERS
OF NATURE

To kick things off, get ready to meet some of the coolest critters and the most puzzling plants our world has to offer. In this chapter, we'll discover animals with accents, immortal jellyfish, glow-in-the-dark magic, record-breaking trees, and some *really* gross flowers.

AMAZING ANIMAL FACTS

Penguin Proposals: Penguins are more than just tuxedo-wearing birds. When a penguin wants to ask another penguin to be their partner, they give them a pebble. It's a token of their affection, similar to the way we exchange rings.

Surfing Ducks: Ducks aren't just about swimming in ponds. Some ducks have been spotted riding the waves and seem to enjoy it!

Walking Doggie: There's a brave dog named Dexter who learned to walk on his hind legs after his front legs got hurt. He's a real trooper and strolls around his neighbourhood alongside his human family. Dexter is a four-legged inspiration.

Dragonfly Love: Dragonflies are not only agile fliers but also romantic insects. When dragonflies mate, they form their bodies and tails into a shape that looks like a heart.

Talkative Cats: Cats have a unique way of communication. While they don't meow much to other cats, they do meow a lot when they want to talk to humans. What are they trying to tell us?

Elephant Pacifiers: Baby elephants have a charming habit. They sometimes suck on their trunks for comfort, similar to how you might suck your thumb. It's their way of soothing themselves.

Octopus Marvel: The giant Pacific octopus is quite the marvel of the ocean. It has not one, not two, but three hearts! Plus, it has nine brains, and its blood is actually blue. It's like an extraterrestrial creature from our own oceans.

Ticklish Rats: You might not think of rats as ticklish, but guess what? Scientists found that when they tickle rats on their backs, the rats make noises that seem to be laughter. Although these sounds are much squeakier than a human laugh.

Daddy Seahorses: You know how mums often take care of babies? Well, in the sea world, seahorse dads do that job! Male seahorses carry the babies in a special pouch on their bellies until they're ready to be born.

Squirrel Gardeners: Squirrels are nature's gardeners in a way. They bury acorns in the ground to save them for later snacks, but sometimes they forget where they've hidden them. Those forgotten acorns end up sprouting into big, leafy trees!

Cows and Music: Cows are fans of music just like us! When they listen to calm and soothing tunes, they make more milk. And guess what? They love R.E.M's song 'Everybody Hurts' the most.

Caring Puppies: When boy puppies play with girl puppies, they sometimes let the girls win, even if they're stronger. It's like their mum's told them to 'play nicely'.

Inmates and Animals: Imagine prisoners helping to raise guide dogs! There's a special program where inmates get to train these dogs. In another cool prison program, 'death row' cats find new pals in prisoners. The cats, dogs and inmates all get a fresh start by helping each other out.

Turtle Trick: Turtles have a pretty unique skill. They can breathe through their butts!

Otter Sleepover: Sea otters are the ultimate buddies. They hold hands while they snooze to make sure they don't drift apart.

Cow Pals: Cows are social creatures too. They have best friends they hang out with a lot. They do stuff like groom each other, play around, and share chill spots. Cow friendships are truly moo-ving!

Remarkable Regrowth: The axolotl is a salamander from Mexico, which looks like a cute cartoon. It has the amazing power of being able to regrow almost all its body parts if it's injured, including its limbs, heart, spinal cord and brain!

OCTO-WHAT?!

Octopuses are fantastic gardeners of the sea. They gather sponges and natural materials on the ocean floor to put around their homes. Also, some deep sea Octopuses have been shown to sit on their eggs for up to four and a half years! This is because it takes a long time for the eggs to develop in the freezing deep-sea temperatures. Sometimes hundreds of octopuses gather together in areas with hot springs, to create special deep-sea nurseries where their eggs hatch faster.

Cross-Species BFFs: Animals don't just make friends within their own kind. Animals like chimpanzees, horses, elephants, dolphins, and whales can also become buddies with other types of animals.

Chimpanzee Cheers: Just like people, chimpanzees seem to have a taste for adventure. Some chimpanzees in the jungle like to find ripe fruits that have fermented, turning into something like jungle alcohol. Now that's a truly wild party.

Moo Variations: Cows have their own cow accents! Just like how people from different places sound a bit different when they talk, cows from small groups have their unique way of mooing.

PUZZLING PLANTS

Secret Plant Talk: Guess what? Plants can talk to each other! Well, not with words, but through special chemical signals. When a plant is being attacked by insects, it sends out these signals into the air to warn nearby plants. It's like they're saying, 'Hey, danger ahead!' So, the other plants can get ready and protect themselves too.

Moving Plants: Picture this – a plant that moves when you touch it! The sensitive plant, also known as Mimosa pudica, has leaves that quickly fold inward if you touch or disturb them. This helps them stay safe from any potential danger.

Purple Carrots: Carrots might be orange now, but they weren't always that way. In the past, carrots were actually purple! Farmers started breeding orange carrots in the Netherlands in the sixteenth century, in honour of King William of Orange.

Doomsday Seed Vault: In case of a big food shortage emergency, there's a special place called the 'Svalbard Global Seed Vault' or 'Doomsday Seed Vault' in Norway. It's like a super safe storage vault for ancient seeds that can survive tough conditions. These seeds are kept to save us if conditions on planet Earth get really challenging. Let's hope humans never have to use them.

Glowing Plants: Have you ever seen a mushroom that glows in the dark? Well, some fungi, like the ghost fungus, have an incredible power called bioluminescence. They can produce light without making any heat. They basically have their own little night light. Scientists think it may attract insects and help them spread reproductive spores, or it may just be an accident!

Stinky Plants: Did you know that some plants are really good at pretending? Take the corpse flower, for example. It's a sneaky plant that mimics the smell of rotting flesh. Yuck! There's another stinky plant called the carrion plant. It's edible, but it has such a horrible smell that scientists are trying to use it to help people who want to suppress their appetite. Another one called the dead horse lily even looks like an animal's behind! These pongy plants attract flies and beetles that like those kinds of smells. Once the bugs are inside, they get covered in pollen, and when they leave, they help fertilise other flowers.

GIANT FLOWER ALERT!

That corpse flower you just learnt about. Well, it's the king of flowers. Its scientific name is Rafflesia arnoldii and it grows in Indonesia! The flowers are huge, reaching over one metre (3.3 feet) in diameter.

The 'Ugly' Orchid: Did you know that plants can be beautiful in their own unique way? But there's an orchid called Gastrodia agnicellus that some people consider the 'ugliest' plant on our planet and has been described as 'brown, fleshy and grotesque'. It was discovered by a brilliant botanist in a rainforest in Madagascar. But even the unattractive plants deserve love for helping other species to survive.

Hungry Plants: Imagine plants that eat insects! Some special plants, like the Venus flytrap, have cleverly developed the ability to catch and digest small bugs. They do this because they live in places where they don't get many nutrients from the soil.

Tall Fungi Mystery: Before s, there were some giant creatures called Prototaxites. They looked like trees, but they were actually fungi! These mysterious beings grew trunks as wide as one metre (three feet) and as tall as eight metres (26 feet). Scientists had a big debate about them, but a study in 2007 confirmed they were not trees, but fascinating fungi.

400K AND COUNTING....

Our planet is bursting with plant diversity. Can you believe there are over 400,000 species of plants out there? And guess what? Scientists keep discovering new ones every year.

Forests in Trouble: Our beautiful forests need our help. Sadly, 80% of Earth's original forests have been destroyed. And because of this, Mother Nature is responding with climate change. It's a reminder for us to take care of our planet and protect its green treasures.

ID Confusion: Did you know that pumpkins and avocados are fruits? Why? Because they have developed from the flowers of plants and contain seeds. And guess what? Pineapples are berries! It gets even trickier – rhubarb is a vegetable, and cucumber is a fruit too. Mind-boggling.

Plant Hotspots: Did you know that more than half of all plant species come from just five countries? These botanical hotspots are Brazil, Colombia, China, Indonesia, and Australia. There are so many different habitats in these nations that diversity rules!

Not on the Menu: Even though there are tons of plant species, we humans tend to stick to just a few when it comes to our meals. Out of the 400,000 edible plant species, we mostly eat around 200 of them. Rice, maize, and wheat are famous plants that provide us with a big chunk of our food.

Nature's Compass: Plants can be our guides in the wild! In northern temperate climates, moss tends to grow more on the northern side of tree trunks. So if you ever get lost in the woods, just follow the moss compass. And here's another trick – tree rings can also help you. Thicker rings on the southern side of a tree in the northern hemisphere and vice versa can tell you which way is which.

Plant Sibling Love: Plants can recognize their own siblings, just like you do with your brothers and sisters. They even treat their siblings nicely by competing less for resources like space to grow. It's like they have special family bonds.

Caffeine, the Plant Protector: Plants like coffee beans, tea, and cacao produce caffeine to keep pesky insects away, acting like a toxic shield that paralyses and kills those bugs. Caffeine is also harmful to birds, dogs, cats, and some other critters. It's a secret weapon in the plant world.

Sinister Smiles: Ever heard of the Hemlock Water-Dropwort plant? It's a bit of a troublemaker. It's very poisonous, and when people come in contact with it, it can also cause their facial muscles to contort, giving them a creepy smile! Don't worry, it's not a permanent grin.

Dumb Cane Drama: Imagine a plant called 'Mother-In-Law's Tongue' or 'Dumb Cane.' It's not because it can't talk, but because its toxic sap can make your tongue swell up and even take away your voice. Yikes! It can have the same effect on our furry friends, dogs, and cats. Let's stay away from this one!

Tomatoes and Potatoes Together: Imagine a plant that grows both tomatoes and potatoes at the same time! It's called the 'Ketchup 'n' Fries' or 'Tomtato' plant. Isn't that cool? You can have delicious tomatoes and yummy potatoes from just one plant.

Happy Bananas: Eating bananas can make you feel happy. It's true! Bananas have a special natural chemical that can boost your mood and make you smile. So next time you're feeling down, grab a banana and let it work its magic. It's just a strange coincidence that they're also smile-shaped …

PLANT S.O.S

The smell of freshly cut grass is like a secret message from the plants. They release special chemicals called 'green leaf volatiles' or 'GLVs' to let nearby plants and creatures know that they are under attack. It's like their way of saying, 'Hey, something's not right here!' This can help other creatures decide if it's a good time for them to hide or to hunt, and nearby plants may start their defence strategy. Although we humans can't detect these signals, plants are communicating with each other all the time.

Taste Test Challenge: Apples, potatoes, and onions definitely don't taste the same, right? Well, here's a fun challenge – try eating them with your nose closed! When you can't smell them, you might discover that they actually taste quite similar. Now there's a delicious mystery for you to solve.

Fungal Surprise: Hold onto your hats for a surprising fact – fungi, like mushrooms, are more related to animals than plants! Fungi and animals share a common history and have a very useful molecule called lanosterol that plants don't have.

TERRIFIC TREES

Tree Tales: There are about three trillion trees in the world. They make habitats beautiful, from big forests to city streets. But, uh-oh, sometimes people chop down forests for quick gains, not thinking about the long-term effects like climate change and less wildlife. Earth used to have a lot more trees, but over the past 12,000 years, we've lost 46% of them. A lot of this is related to humans clearing land for farming. Luckily, scientists are working hard to help us use trees wisely and protect our precious forests and everything that calls them home, but we all need to find ways to bring back those leafy friends and make our planet greener again.

Earth Before Trees: Let's take a trip back in time when trees didn't exist. Can you believe that for most of Earth's history, there were no trees at all? It wasn't until around 470 million years ago that plants started to colonise land, but they were small guys like mosses and liverworts without deep roots. The big and tall trees we know came much later. Lucky they did, or we wouldn't be here!

Ancient Ginkgo Tree: Meet the wise old Ginkgo biloba tree. It's one of the oldest living tree species on our planet. Members of the Gingko family first appeared about 270 million years ago, before the dinosaurs even existed! The modern surviving version of ginkgo has been around for a mind-blowing 170 million years.

Dinosaur-Era Trees: Imagine trees that lived when dinosaurs roamed the Earth! During the Jurassic Period, there were amazing cone-bearing evergreen trees called Wollemia. They were thought to be extinct for 150 million years, but guess what? In 1994, a few survivors of one species were found in Australia's Wollemia National Park. It's like finding a living fossil! These special trees are critically endangered, so we need to protect them.

Towering Tree: Have you ever seen a tree that touches the sky? Well, there's a coastal redwood called Hyperion that holds the record for being the tallest tree in the whole world! It stands at an incredible 115 metres (379 feet) tall and lives in Redwood National Park in California. That's as high as a 35-storey building! But that's not the all-time record. In Australia, there was once a eucalyptus tree that reached a towering height of 130 metres (435 feet). That's like having a skyscraper made of leaves and bark!

Smart Tree Communication: Did you know that trees can communicate with each other? They're not just standing there, they're sending invisible chemical signals through the air! When a tree is under attack by insects, it releases chemicals that warn nearby trees to be prepared. Some trees even call in backup by attracting helpful predators and parasites. Trees also stay connected via an incredible underground network. Their roots have a special relationship with fungi called mycorrhizal fungi. The fungi help trees absorb more water and nutrients, and in return, the trees share sugars. But it's not just a one-on-one connection – entire forests are connected too! Older 'mother trees' send nutrients to young seedlings through this network. They're a big family helping each other survive and grow.

Oxygen Heroes: Trees make our lives possible with their oxygen production! They provide us with fresh air to breathe. While phytoplankton (microscopic plants) in the ocean also contribute, trees are a major source of oxygen on land. Some people say that a mature leafy tree can produce enough oxygen for a few people each year. But even if the numbers are hazy, one thing is clear – trees do so much for us! They provide shade, food, and even help clean up air pollution. What would we do without them?

Tree Homes for Wildlife: A lot of animals call trees home. From squirrels and songbirds to bats and bees, many creatures find shelter and food there. Did you know that adding just one tree to an open pasture can increase the number of bird species from almost zero to as high as 80? Trees create important habitats, supporting a wide variety of wildlife. They're like nature's apartment blocks, housing biodiversity and bringing joy to our world.

Deadliest Tree: The manchineel tree in Florida comes with a serious warning label. It's fruit is deadly, and even just standing under it during a rainstorm can give you blisters. if you try to burn it, the smoke can make you go temporarily blind! Yikes, better stay away from that one!

Exploding Trees: The wild sandbox tree, aka the "Dynamite Tree." is covered in spikes, has toxic sap, and get this – its fruit can explode! Boom! When those fruits burst open, they shoot seeds like tiny missiles at 150 miles per hour.

Lucky Trees: Way back in ancient times, the Celts were all about trees being home to friendly spirits. They believed that if you gave a tree a little knock, it would wake up its guardian spirit, like a tree superhero! And that's how saying "knock on wood" for good luck began. Cool, right?

Pencils Galore: Guess what? A single average-size tree can make enough wood to create a whopping 170,100 pencils!

Lightning Lovers: Oak trees have a shocking secret! They get struck by lightning more than any other tree. It's like they have a special connection to the thunder and lightning in the sky. So if you're ever caught in a storm, find shelter away from those lightning-loving oaks.

19

LONGEST LIVES

Time to dive into the world of super-old animals! Some glass sponges (yep, sponges are animals!) found in the East China Sea and Southern Ocean are estimated to be over 10,000 years old. They might be the oldest living animals on Earth.

Wise Old Bird: Cocky Bennett, an Australian sulphur-crested cockatoo, lived to be 120 years old. He travelled the world and had some amazing phrases up his feathery sleeve. Imagine having a bird friend that could talk and tell stories! His favourite sentences were 'one feather more and I'll fly' and 'one at a time, gentlemen, please'.

Spider Survivor: Are you ready for a creepy-crawly record? Number 16, a female Gaius villosus armoured trapdoor spider, lived for a mind-boggling 43 years.

Mighty Mouse: Brace yourself for a small but mighty record-holder! Patrick Stewart, the mouse (yes, named after the iconic actor), holds the title for the oldest living mouse ever. As of 9 February 2023, he reached the impressive age of 9 years and 210 days!

Purrfectly Old Cat: Get ready to meet the oldest cat ever recorded! Creme Puff, owned by Jake Perry from Texas, lived a fantastic life. She celebrated her 38th birthday, which is like 169 cat years! That's a lot of napping and cuddles.

Time-Travelling Tortoise: Prepare to meet a tortoise that might hold the record for the oldest terrestrial animal ever! Adwaita, an Aldabra giant tortoise, lived an estimated 255 years. Slow and steady wins the race.

20

ANCIENT PLANTS

Ancient Tree Champions: Trees can be real conquerors of ageing. Imagine a tree that's older than the pyramids in Egypt. Well, the bristlecone pine tree in California is exactly that. It's a whopping 4,855 years old! That's like having a tree friend that has seen more birthdays than everyone you know put together.

Super Old Tree Communities: While the bristlecone pine tree is an ancient individual, there are whole communities of trees called clonal trees that have been alive for over 80,000 years! Being clonal means they share the same genetic code and so are almost like a single being. One such amazing group of 50,000 aspen trees is called Pando. They have been spreading and growing together for thousands and thousands of years. In the Mojave Desert in California, a creosote bush named King Clone reigns supreme. It's estimated to be a mind-blowing 11,700 years old.

Fungal Wonder: Deep underground in Oregon's Malheur National Forest, there's a hidden giant called the 'Humongous Fungus.' It's a clonal subterranean fungus, and scientists believe it's between 2,000 and 8,500 years old! It's not just old but also the largest organism in the world, covering an area as big as 9.5 km² (2,384 acres).

Grandmother Yew Tree: Picture a wise and ancient tree standing tall in a little village in Wales. The Llangernyw Yew has been around for a mind-boggling 4,000 to 5,000 years! That's older than your great-great-great-great-great-great-grandparents!

Seagrass Time Traveler: Now let's head down to the Australian coast near Shark Bay, where we'll find a huge colony of sea grass called Posidonia australis. This incredible plant has been growing for over 4,500 years, making it one of the oldest living plants on Earth!

IMMORTAL JELLYFISH

Imagine a jellyfish so small, it's only three millimetres in diameter. That's like the size of a little bead! But don't let its small size fool you, because these jellyfish have an amazing party trick. When these tiny creatures get hurt or are super hungry, they can do something incredible – they can turn back time! It's like they have their own Doctor Who-style powers of regeneration. They can roll back their biological clock and become young again. That means, in theory, they could live forever!

These immortal jellyfish, also known as Turritopsis dohrnii, have been floating through the oceans for a super long time. We're talking way before the dinosaurs went extinct, like 66 million years ago! It's mind-blowing to think that a single jellyfish could have been alive for that entire time.

Although it's technically possible for these jellyfish to live forever, it's not something scientists can prove just yet. They have only been studying these jellyfish since the 1980s, so they don't have centuries of data. This fascinating puzzle is something that scientists are still working on.

Even though these immortal jellyfish have amazing powers, they still have to watch out for enemies. Predators like fish, sharks, turtles, and even other jellyfish can easily gobble them up. So, they probably won't take over the world anytime soon!

INCREDIBLE ANIMAL ABILITIES

THE BLOB

Let's talk about a mysterious creature called 'The Blob.' It's not your ordinary plant or fungus, and scientists are still trying to figure out exactly what it is. The bizarre life form was discovered in France, at the Paris Zoological Park, looking 'like a fungus, but acting like an animal.'This yellowish blob can change its appearance, sometimes looking like a plant, a mushroom, or even mucus. It's like a master of disguise! But that's not all. The Blob has some super cool powers. It can move without legs or wings, and get this, it has 720 different sexes! Wow! Even though The Blob doesn't have a brain, it can learn. It can find its way through mazes to get food and even figure out how to avoid lines of salt that it doesn't like. And get this, if two Blobs come together, the one that has learned something can teach the other one. So cool!

Next, we have the **shape-shifting frogs!** Imagine finding a frog that can change its shape and texture. Scientists discovered a special kind of frog called the mutable rain frog in Ecuador. These frogs can transform their skin from rough and spiny to smooth in just a few minutes. That's some disguise! There's another cool frog called the Sobetes robber frog that can shape-shift too. Who knows, maybe there are even more shape-shifting creatures out there waiting to be discovered!

Did you know that animals can tell the time? Scientists have discovered that animals, just like us, have internal clocks. These clocks are made up of special neurons in their brains that turn on and off! That's why pet cats and dogs always know exactly when it's dinner time!

EXTRAORDINARY DOGS

Dogs have an insane sense of smell. Their noses are way more powerful than ours, like up to a hundred times stronger! They can even 'smell' heat, like the warmth coming from someone's body. Isn't that amazing? You know what's even cooler? Dogs can still find their way and hunt even when their eyesight, hearing, or smell isn't as sharp as before. That's because they can sniff out the heat from their prey. Scientists discovered this mind-blowing ability by testing dogs with MRI scanners. They found out that dogs can detect even really tiny amounts of heat.

Our canine friends have another incredible power called magnetoreception. It means they can sense the Earth's weak magnetic field, just like some birds and other animals can. It's like they have a built-in compass! Maybe dogs can use their magnetoreception to find new paths or find their way back home. With the help of science, we'll soon find out.

NOW ON TO SOME REAL LIFE WONDER DOGS...

First, we have **Jess, the super-smart Jack Russell** from England. One day, Jess's owner, Rebecca, was having a really bad asthma attack and couldn't breathe properly. But guess what? Jess sensed the danger and ran to Rebecca's room to get her inhaler. Talk about a best friend! But it didn't end there. Rebecca wanted to check if it was just luck, so she hid her inhaler and coughed a little. And you know what? Jess found the hidden inhaler and brought it back to her owner!

TEXAS S.O.S

In Texas, there's a dog named Chrome who is a real hero. One night, Chrome's owner, Laura, and her two boys were sleeping when Chrome woke Laura up. Can you guess why? Well, their house was on fire! Chrome stayed with Laura and made sure she realised what was happening. Then, Chrome zoomed off to get the two boys to safety. Thanks to Chrome's quick thinking, everyone got out of the house before it got engulfed in flames. Wow!

24

RUBY TO THE RESCUE...

In New York, there's a pit bull named Ruby with a similar sense for danger. One night, Ruby started barking like crazy for a really long time. Ronene and Chris, Ruby's owners, knew something was up because Ruby is usually such a good and well-trained dog. So they investigated and sniffed the air. Guess what they found? The smell of propane! They realised it was coming from their new heater, which could have caused deadly carbon monoxide poisoning. Thanks to Ruby's super sniffing skills and intuition, they all got out of the house safely. Phew!

Now, let's talk about Todd, the golden retriever from Arizona. Todd and his owner, Paula, were hiking when they came across a rattlesnake on the path. Eek! But Todd didn't hesitate for a second. He jumped in front of Paula just as the rattlesnake was about to strike, and he got bitten on his snout. Ouch! Paula rushed Todd to the animal hospital, and luckily, he made a full recovery. That's loyalty!

In Central Queensland, Australia, another amazing dog saved the day. A 56-year-old man was riding his quad bike on a rural property when he had an accident and got trapped underneath it. Guess who came to the rescue? His faithful cattle dog! The man was stuck there all night, but the dog cuddled up to him to keep him warm. A neighbour on a horse spotted the overturned quad bike and called for help. The man was airlifted to the hospital, and his saviour dog went along too.

There was a super tiny toy poodle named Pickle in North Carolina, US. One morning, out of nowhere, a big aggressive bear burst through the door of the house! Can you imagine? Pickle's owner, Tiffany, screamed for her kids to stay safe, and she hid behind the couch. But Pickle didn't back down! He bravely distracted the bear and led it outside. They fought like champions, but sadly, Pickle got hurt too badly and didn't make it. He saved his family's life, though!

Kabang is one brave dog! At home in the Philippines, she saved two kids from a speedy motorbike and got hurt in the process. But her owner, Rudi, made sure she got better. Their bond is unbreakable, even after all that excitement.

Now, let's go to Canada, where a wonderful dog named Noah showed his amazing instincts. His owner, Jane, has a lung disease and relies on an oxygen tank to breathe. One night, Jane wasn't feeling well, so she decided to sleep on the couch downstairs. But in the morning, she collapsed and passed out! That's when Noah sprang into action. He ran upstairs and barked like crazy at Jane's husband, Ken, to wake him up. Ken quickly realised something was wrong and called for help. Jane had pneumonia, which combined with her lung disease, could have been ultra dangerous. But thanks to Noah's action and Ken's quick thinking, Jane got the help she needed just in time.

DARING DOGGY HERO

Far north in Alaska, there's a special dog named Nanook who is making heroic rescues. His owner, Scott Swift, lives near a long trail called the Crow Pass Trail. Nanook loves following hikers and knows the whole route by heart. One day, a student named Amelia was hiking alone when she slipped and fell down a big icy mountain. Uh-oh! But guess who came to her rescue? It was Nanook! He stayed by her side and guided her back to the trail. But the adventure wasn't over yet. Amelia slipped again while crossing a river. But Nanook was there to save her again! He helped her get to safety and even kept her awake by licking her face until a rescue helicopter arrived.

After saving Amelia, Nanook became a real star and started rescuing other hikers too! At least, there were three other rescues that his owner, Scott, knew about. But Scott wanted to find even more people who were helped by Nanook. So he started a special social media page to share their stories. Within just a few days, tons of rescue stories started popping up! Nanook had been saving more people than anyone ever imagined. What a superstar! But here's the most mind-blowing part: Nanook wasn't even trained to be a rescue dog! He was adopted from an 'adopt-a-pet' event in a shopping centre car park. It just goes to show that heroes can come from unexpected places.

TOP 10 SURVIVORS OF EVOLUTION

Ginkgo Trees: Ginkgo trees are living fossils, rocking it for over 175 million years. They even hung out with dinosaurs back in the day. The modern ones look almost identical to their ancient ancestors – talk about a timeless style!

Crocodylians: You might think of crocs as ancient, and you'd be right! These guys have been around for an astounding 205 million years, even hanging out with dinosaurs. There are all sorts of croc species, from huge predators to smaller ones, and they've been through it all.

Duck-billed Platypus: This mammal is a true weirdo in the best way. It lays eggs but has a duck's snout and a beaver-like tail. Platypuses belong to a group called monotremes, which goes back over 175 million years. Fossils in Australia suggest they had platypus-like relatives 110 million years ago!

Cow Sharks: Sharks are way older than you'd think. Some, like cow sharks with their unique six or seven gills, are like time travellers from the deep sea. They've been around for at least 175 million years, scavenging on marine leftovers and later munching on marine mammals.

Coelacanth: These fish were thought to be extinct, but they made a comeback! Coelacanths have been around for a staggering 400 million years. They're distant cousins of humans and have unique fins with bones like our limbs.

Horsetails: Now, let's give some love to plants! Horsetails have been hanging out for over 350 million years. They used to rule forests before today's trees took over. And guess what? The coal we use today is the ancient remains from the time when these ancient plants were the kings of the forest.

Lice: Yep, even tiny, annoying, insects have epic survival stories. Lice have been around for 115-130 million years, living on mammals since the time of feathered dinosaurs. Just think about those ancient lice-making dinosaurs itch!

Velvet Worms: Don't let the name fool you – these aren't really worms. They're more like ancient cousins of insects. Velvet worms have been crawling around for a mind-blowing 505 million years! Scientists have found fossils of these critters in the famous Burgess Shale – a fossil-rich area of mountain in Canada.

Brachiopods: These are shelled creatures with a deep history, going back over 530 million years. They've seen oceans change, and their unique way of living, generally attached to the sea floor, sets them apart from other sea creatures.

Horseshoe Crab: Last but not least, meet the horseshoe crab. They've been around for nearly 480 million years! These arthropods might look prehistoric, with their spiky tails and hard shells, but they've adapted and thrived through the ages.

UNLIKELY ANIMAL FRIENDSHIPS

Meet Mark and Agee, the unlikely pals. Agee is a huge polar bear, born and raised by staff in a Swedish wildlife park. She and Mark do all sorts of fun stuff together. They dive into the pool and even snuggle up in bed! Agee lives with Mark all year round, and they're inseparable. It's sad that Agee was born into captivity, but beautiful that such a strong friendship came from the situation

Dindim the penguin and Joao are like best buddies. When Dindim was in a bad way – all oily and hungry on a beach near Rio de Janeiro, Brazil – Joao came to the rescue. He took really good care of Dindim and made sure he was okay. And guess what? Dindim comes back to hang out with Joao for about eight months every year. That's some serious friendship!

Kwibi the gorilla and Damian Aspinall have a heartwarming story. Damian is a conservationist, and Kwibi was born in his wildlife park in rural England, but then released into the wild with six other young gorillas. They were apart for five long years, but when they finally met again, it was a big reunion. Kwibi introduced Damian to her gorilla family, and it was super touching.

Pocho the crocodile and fisherman Chito are like the coolest duo ever. Chito found Pocho lying very sick on a riverbank in Costa Rica. Chito took care of Pocho and then released him back into the river, but Pocho returned! They later did awesome performances together that everyone loved.

Derrick Thompson and baby elephant Kham Lha are total pals. One day in northern Thailand Kham Lha thought Derrick was drowning and rushed to help him. She supported and sheltered him in the water with her trunk and body. Derrick works really hard to protect elephants, and Kham Lha loves him for it.

Christian the lion had quite the journey. He was bought from a London store by John and Ace and grew up in their apartment. They knew he didn't belong in the city and let him go back to the wild. But when they visited Africa, something unexpected happened – Christian remembered them! It was a heartwarming reunion between friends.

SOMETIMES ANIMALS FIND THEIR BEST FRIEND IN ANOTHER SPECIES...

Picture a young monkey in China who was left all alone on an island by his mum. His life was pretty hard until he made an unexpected friend – a pigeon! Now, these two buddies are always together, and their friendship is something really unique.

Here's the story of Albert the sheep and Themba the elephant from a wildlife centre in South Africa. At first, Themba was like, 'Go away, Albert!' But then, something amazing happened – they became best pals! They nap together, take walks, and even learn cool stuff from each other. Albert even figured out how to eat thorny bushes, just like Themba.

In England, there's Snowy the cat and Gladys the hen, and they're breaking all the rules of the cat-and-bird game. Gladys had a run-in with a fox, but luckily, Snowy came to the rescue. Now, they're like family, grooming each other and playing together. Their bond is super strong.

Mi-Lu the deer was born in a safari park in the UK but didn't have a mum. Guess who stepped in? Geoffrey and Kipper, two dogs! They took care of Mi-Lu like he was their own, and they became a unique little family until Mi-Lu was old enough to be released to live with his deer family.

Imagine this: Owen the baby hippo and Mzee the 130-year-old giant tortoise became buddies after Owen separated from his family in the tsunami in December 2004. He was relocated to the rescue centre in Kenya where Mzee was living. Now, they're like peas in a pod, hanging out, eating together, and have their own books, website and musical!

When Lazarus the tiny chihuahua was left without a mum, Jada the cat stepped up. Jada already had kittens so it was a mixed-up family, but everyone got along great. Lazarus grew up healthy and happy thanks to his furry feline mum.

UNUSAL PREHISTORIC CREATURES

Deinocheirus: Deinocheirus is a dinosaur that leaves us with a big question mark. All we have are two enormous arms, each eight feet long, and they belonged to a dinosaur that could have been around 12 metres (40 feet) long! No one knows for sure what these giant arms were for. Some think they were for tearing apart other dinosaurs, while others say they were more for defence. There's even a crazy idea that it used these huge arms to climb trees!.

Deinotherium, The Ancient Tusker: Imagine an elephant, but super-sized with two big chin tusks! These massive animals were some of the largest mammals ever, standing about 3.5–4.5 metres (12–15 feet) tall. They used their unique tusks to dig up roots and plants, making them different from today's elephants.

Nyctosaurus: Pterosaurs, like Nyctosaurus, were already unusual, but this one stood out even more. Unlike most pterosaurs, it didn't have claws on its wings. It looked a bit like other pterosaurs, but a new species found in 2003 had a massive, antler-like crest on its head. Some thought there might be a flap between these antlers for flying, but others weren't so sure. It's a bit of a mystery!

Epidexipteryx: This feathered oddity is a small dinosaur that lived a long time ago. Even though it couldn't fly, it had four long tail feathers, kind of like fancy decorations. It was only about 25 centimetres (10 inches) tall, like a pigeon. What's super interesting is that this little dinosaur shows that feathers existed millions of years before flying did!

A GIANT MYSTERY...

Amphicoelias fragillimus: Scientists have only discovered one piece of the backbone, but it's enormous. Just this one piece is 1.5 metres (five feet) tall! Estimates suggest it might have been one of the biggest creatures ever, perhaps measuring up to 40 metres. However, the fossil disappeared without a trace, leaving us to wonder if it was a giant or just a tall tale. The truth remains a mystery!

Epidendrosaurus: Here's another bird-like dinosaur, but this one was a tree-dweller. It had an extra-long third finger, like built-in chopsticks. Scientists think it might have been used to grab insects. How cool is that?

Microraptor: Picture a dinosaur that could glide through the air with not two, but four wings! Microraptors looked like birds but couldn't fly like the ones today. It was a bit of a mystery but is a key link between birds and dinosaurs. There was even a time when a fake fossil of Microraptor made the news, causing quite a stir!

Therizinosauridaes: They were herbivores, which means they ate plants, not meat. They had long necks and huge claws, making them look quite unusual among meat-eating dinosaurs. Some even had feathers, making them even more intriguing. One, called Therizinosaurus, is a bit of a mystery because we only have a few fossils, but its gigantic claws, about a metre long, really stand out!

Tanystropheus: The Remarkable Long-Necker: When you hear 'long-necked,' you might think of long-necked dinosaurs or sea creatures, but Tanystropheus was different. It was a reptile from a long time ago with a three-metre (10-foot) neck! It probably liked to eat fish and might have lived near the water, using its long neck to catch fish.

Sharovipteryx: The Leap-Glider: Sharovipteryx was another ancient glider like Microraptor, but it had an interesting twist. It had 'wings' on both its front and back legs. These likely helped it jump around and glide. Some people even thought it could be related to pterosaurs, the flying reptiles, but its unique wings raised questions about that idea.

Pterodaustro: Pterodaustro was a special kind of flying reptile with teeth that were similar to the ones found in some whales. It used these teeth to munch on small water creatures, just like flamingos eat brine shrimp. And who knows, like flamingos, it might have had a pinkish tint too!

Stethacanthus: Sharks are cool, and Stethacanthus was no exception. It had a unique anvil-shaped fin on its back with small spikes. It also had a strange growth on its head, which made it look quite different from your regular shark. Scientists think this unusual fin might have had something to do with finding mates or defence, making it even more interesting.

Helicoprion: Imagine finding a fossil that looks like a spiral shell but turns out to be a spiral of shark teeth. That's Helicoprion! Scientists couldn't agree on where this toothy spiral belonged in the shark's mouth. Some said the tip of the lower jaw, and some said the tail or even the snout. It was a real mystery!

Longisquama: Feathers or Scales? Longisquama, a small creature from the time of dinosaurs, has a little mystery around it. It seems to have had long feathers on its back, suggesting that birds might not have come from meat-eating dinosaurs. Some think these 'feathers' could be special scales or even just plant fronds that got fossilised with it.

Dunkleosteus: Imagine a fish from your wildest ocean nightmares. Dunkleosteus was a massive, armoured fish that reached up to 10 metres (33 feet) long and had one of the strongest bites ever. Instead of regular teeth, it had a sort of beak to chomp on its prey. Swimming near this creature in ancient times would have been pretty scary!

BEING HUMAN

We explore the quirks, wonders, and peculiarities that make us, well, us. From the incredible capabilities of our brains to the funny habits we share, get ready for a journey into the amazing world of humanity – where every fact is as unique as the individuals reading this book.

FRIENDSHIP AND KINDNESS

Your friends are not only fun but also really good for your body and mind. Scientists discovered that having friends makes us healthier, and happier, and even helps us live longer

Most people make almost 400 friendships over their lifetime! But guess what? Out of those many friendships, only about 33 of them stay strong over time. And out of those, we have about six super close friends who feel like family.

When we help others, our brains light up with happiness. Scientists found that giving to others makes us feel even happier than buying things for ourselves. That could be giving in any way, whether it's our time, support or a mega-delicious chocolate cake. Our brains release a special chemical called oxytocin, which makes us feel all warm and fuzzy inside when we're kind.

Did you know that people who don't have a lot of money often give the most? Amazingly, people who don't earn much are often the ones who share their money to help others in need.

Ever had a day when you felt super tired and not in the best mood? Well, turns out, how well you've slept can affect how kind you feel. When we're tired, we might not feel as eager to help others. It's like our kindness meter gets a bit low when we're sleepy.

When we do something nice for others, it can start a chain reaction of more kindness. It's like tossing a pebble into a pond and watching the ripples spread. And fortunately, when we're kind and give to others, people are more likely to be kind back to us.

GENEROUS FOLK

Chuck Feeney's Quiet Kindness: Once upon a time, there was a really wealthy guy named Chuck Feeney. He had a whopping $4 billion US dollars! But guess what he did? He started secretly giving away most of his money to help people. He helped clinics for people with AIDS, healthcare in Cuba, and other important things around the world. His motto was to give while he was still alive, and he said something wise: 'Money is attractive, but you can't wear two pairs of shoes at once.'

Taxi Driver's Honesty: Mukul Asaduzzaman, a regular taxi driver in New York City, became famous for being honest. He returned a huge $21,000 US dollars that a grandma from Italy left in his taxi. There are stories of other taxi drivers being just as generous, giving free rides to people who are struggling with money or giving back lost money to passengers. Kindness is even more amazing when you don't have a lot to give.

Super Donors: Imagine people donating their organs, like kidneys, not to their family, but to complete strangers! It's called 'altruistic kidney donation.' These big-hearted people give a kidney to someone they've never met. They're not just saving lives but also inspiring others to be kind. From a woman giving her kidney to a little girl to a man from one place donating to a woman in a distant city, these stories show that kindness can truly be a lifesaver.

Bill Gates, the Giving Guru: You know the computer genius who made Microsoft? That's Bill Gates! He became the richest person on the planet. But instead of collecting all the money, he's using it to do amazing things. He joined forces with his wife Melinda to create a special foundation to help fight diseases and make sure kids get the medicine they need. Bill Gates gave away a jaw-dropping $58 billion US dollars and decided to share his fortune with charities, not just keep it for his family.

Warren Buffett's Big Heart: Imagine a super-friendly billionaire named Warren Buffett. He did something huge in 2006! He gave away an incredible $31 billion US dollars to the Gates Foundation. But he didn't stop there. He also gave another $6 billion to groups that are saving the Earth and doing other great stuff. He shared most of his $44 billion fortune because he wants to leave a positive mark while he's alive.

QUIRKY ICONS

These days we like to celebrate quirkiness and individuality. Some of the habits in this chapter are harmless eccentricities. Others are downright dangerous and would be illegal nowadays! Who knows what effects they truly had on these famous minds?

Beethoven Makes a Splash: Ludwig van Beethoven, the famous composer, had a pretty dramatic way of working, just like his intense music. Instead of peacefully writing, he'd pace around for a bit, then pour water all over himself, and even on his floor! He thought the cold water made him more creative.

Weird Sir George: Sir George Sitwell was quite a strange character. He was an English writer who liked collecting old stuff. He even made a special gun to shoot wasps! On his farm, he arranged cows in strange patterns just for fun. And when his wife needed help with money problems, he didn't help her, and she ended up in jail.

The Super Inventor: Leonardo da Vinci was a genius artist and inventor. He never went to regular school, but he made all kinds of amazing inventions and tried to figure out how animal bodies work by cutting them up. He even wrote all his notes backwards!

The Father of Toxicology: Paracelsus was an important scientist in the Renaissance period. He believed in making tiny people from human fluids, and he also thought mythical creatures could be real!

Stalin's Odd Habits: Joseph Stalin was the leader of the Soviet Union, and he had some really strange habits. He had this thing where he'd judge people by smelling their poop! Believe it or not, he created a secret department of officers whose job was to check out Mao Zedong's (leader of China at the time) waste! What were their job titles?

Shy Scientist Henry: Henry Cavendish was a very talented and famous scientist who discovered hydrogen. But he was super shy. He only talked to his maid using written notes and tried to avoid meeting women at all costs. He did everything he could to stay away from people.

The Yellow Fever Daredevil: Stubbins Ffirth tried to show that a disease called yellow fever wasn't contagious by putting himself in close contact with sick people. It didn't go so well and he got sick, but he was brave for using himself as a test subject. Luckily we have clinical trials for much safer testing these days!

Charles Dickens' North: Charles Dickens was a famous writer, but he had some quirks. He'd keep combing his hair and looking in the mirror over and over. And he had this thing where he always wanted to face north when he wrote or went to sleep in bed as he believed it improved his creativity.

Poet's Pongy Apples: Friedrich Schiller was this really famous German poet and playwright who lived way back in the 1700s. He had a strange habit that his friends found a bit odd. He used to keep a drawer full of really yucky, rotten apples in his workroom. Why, you ask? Well, he believed that the stinky smell of those decaying apples helped him write better!

Fossil Detective: Mary Anning was famous for finding and putting together old fossils from the ground. She lived during the nineteenth century on the fossil-rich south coast of England called the Jurassic Coast. Some of her contemporaries believed she got struck by lightning when she was a baby, and that's why she was so smart.

Mad Myth Hunter: Athanasius Kircher was interested in all sorts of things, even mythical creatures like mermaids, giants, and dragons. He truly thought they might be real!

Franklin's Air Baths: Benjamin Franklin, one of the founding fathers of the US, had this interesting habit called 'air baths.' Every day, he would open his windows and let the fresh air into his room while he walked or sat around with no clothes on. He believed his 'air baths' made him feel healthier and more energetic!

THE NOSELESS ASTRONOMER

Tycho Brahe was an astronomer who had a fight and lost his nose! He had a special nose made of copper instead. Just imagine that big shiny metal nose! He also had a pet elk, loved to throw big parties and had his very own court jester.

The Peculiar Thinker: Lady Margaret Cavendish was a philosopher, scientist and writer in the seventeenth century, a time when it was very unusual for women to become famous thinkers. Some people called her 'Mad Madge.' She used to make lists of good and bad qualities of all her friends, which probably didn't make her very popular!

Golden Bathroom Inventor: This guy, Yoshiro Nakamatsu, was a Japanese inventor who thought up ideas underwater. He believed that not having much oxygen made him smarter. Also, his bathroom was all covered in gold to keep out TV and radio waves.

Early Bird Ben: Clockmaker Benjamin Banneker was an engineer and stargazer in the 1700s. He made the first clock all by himself in the US. He loved looking at the stars and planets, and he did it while sitting under a pear tree early in the morning.

Dark-loving William: Harvey William Harvey was a doctor who figured out how our blood flows through our bodies. He had this thing where he liked working in dark, secret places and caves. He thought these extreme places made his ideas better.

The Apocalypse Guy: The famous scientist Isaac Newton loved to study how light and gravity work. He had a serious thing for thinking the world was going to end after the year 2060. He also studied alchemy which involves trying to turn ordinary objects into gold!

Tesla's Odd Habits: Nikola Tesla was an amazing electrical engineer and inventor. He was obsessed with the number three and was terrified of germs. He thought he needed 18 napkins to clean his silverware and glasses because he was so afraid of germs.

The Bean Hater: Pythagoras was a brilliant maths whiz in ancient Greece, but he had a strange dislike for eating beans. He even told his friends they couldn't eat beans either. Some say he thought beans were too special to be eaten.

The Man Who Inspired Frankenstein: Johann Conrad Dippel was born in Castle Frankenstein in 1673. He did some interesting things, like creating a special blue dye and saying he could make a magic potion to live longer by mixing animal parts. Yuck! Some people think he might have inspired the Frankenstein story, but that's still up for debate.

Electric Shock Scientist: Giovanni Aldini was a scientist who lived in the 1800s. He was really into electricity and even used it to try to cure people with mental illnesses. He liked to show off what electricity could do, like making dead animals move with it!

The Dinosaur Eater: William Buckland was a scientist from the 1800s who first described a dinosaur called the Megalosaurus. But here's the twist – he claimed to have eaten some really weird things, like mice, porpoises, and panthers! That's quite an unusual appetite.

POSITIVITY

Here's a whole list of things to be positive about! Positivity can…

Shape Your Brain: Did you know that thinking happy thoughts can change your brain? Your brain builds new paths to be more positive and kicks out those gloomy thoughts.

Enhance Social Life: Being positive not only makes you feel good but also makes your friends happier. You spread joy and make better friendships.

Increase Skill: Being positive can make you even better at what you do! It helps you use your skills and talents to the max.

Aid Learning: When you're positive you open a door to more learning. You become super ready to soak up new stuff and handle any surprises that come your way.

Boost Health: Writing down really good experiences can keep you healthy and less likely to get sick. When you're positive, it's like your body gets a shield against colds and illnesses. You become a germ-fighting machine!

Extend Lifespan: Believe it or not, being positive can help you live longer. They've checked with older folks, and the happy ones tend to stick around for a while!

Support Heart Health: Having a happy attitude is the best medicine for your heart. It keeps it strong and healthy, reducing the chance of heart problems, and even lowers your blood pressure.

You Control Your Positivity: You have the power to be positive! You can kick negativity to the curb, be thankful for the good stuff, and focus on the little moments that make you smile.

LAUGHTER

Catch the Smile Bug: Did you know when we see someone smile or laugh, our brains want to join the fun? Our facial muscles start to make us smile almost automatically. We can catch a case of the giggles just by looking!

Ancient Jokes: Jokes are older than you'd think! There's a joke about 'your mum' that's been around for 3,500 years. People have been cracking the same jokes for centuries.

Laughter Connection: Way back before we even talked, humans used laughter to connect with each other. Believe it or not, even teeny-tiny babies as young as 17 days old can giggle!

Funny Genes: Did you know your sense of humour might be in your genes? Some special genes can make you laugh faster at funny things. It's like having a ticklish spot in your DNA!

Not Just Jokes: Laughter isn't all about jokes and funny stuff. In fact, only a small part of our laughter comes from jokes. Mostly, it's about feeling close to others and being part of a group.

Comedy Marathon: Imagine telling jokes for over eight days straight – that's what a group of comedians did! They set a world record for the longest stand-up comedy show in Nashville, lasting more than eight days!

Parent-Baby Bond: When parents see their baby smiling, a special part of their brain is activated that strengthens their bond with their child.

Laughing Couples: When grown-ups in love laugh together, their hearts get even closer. Couples who share laughs, especially during tough times, have happier and stronger relationships.

43

Calorie Crunch: Here's a funny fact – laughing can help you burn energy! Just 10 to 15 minutes of laughter a day can make your heart race and burn up to 40 calories. It's like having a mini workout while having fun!

Healthy Chuckles: Laughing can help your memory, make your blood vessels work better, boost your immune system, and even help you sleep better. It's like a one-stop shop for feeling good!

The Smiley Power: Did you know that smiles are like magnets? People are drawn to those who smile, and frowns are like 'stay away' signs. People can spot them from far away, and they can even help you get positions in clubs, societies or at work because everyone loves someone who smiles a lot!

Mood Magic: Here's a cool trick: Simply smiling can make you feel better! When you have a big, real smile, it's tough to stay grumpy. It's like a happiness booster!

Endorphin Friends: When you smile, your brain releases something called endorphins. They're like little mood-lifting fairies! Smiling also fights off stress, so you can be a happy camper.

Mighty Muscles: The zygomaticus major and orbicularis oculi are the star muscles of smiling. When they team up, what we get is a genuine smile, known as the 'Duchenne smile'. This is when a smile reaches all the way up to your eyes, making the corners crinkle. Interestingly, a slow-start smile is seen as more sincere.

Emoji Express: You know those cute happy and sad emojis? Different countries show smiles in different ways! Japanese emojis focus on the eyes, while US emojis highlight the mouth.

Blind Smiles: Did you know blind people smile even though they've never seen anyone else smile?

AN UNUSUAL PRESIDENT

Have you heard of José Mujica? He was Uruguay's president from 2010 to 2015, and he was known for being super humble. Here's his story:

José was born in 1935 in Uruguay to a regular, not super-rich family. He got into politics when he was young and even joined a group that wanted to really change things for the better.

When he became president, instead of moving into a fancy mansion, he stayed in his old, not-so-fancy farmhouse outside the capital city. No fancy stuff – just three small rooms for him and his wife, Lucia. He drove an old car, too!

What's especially cool is that José didn't keep all his money. He gave most of his salary to help others and make life better for people who didn't have much. He thought it wasn't right for leaders to lead fancy lives while others struggled.

People loved José because he cared about making things better for everyone. He didn't just talk about it; he did it. He helped poor people, focused on education, and wanted to protect our planet.

Even after being president, José is still a big deal. He showed us that leaders don't need fancy stuff to be great. Being kind, simple, and caring about others is what matters most.

OUR

BODIES

Step into the captivating realm of the human body where the extraordinary meets the everyday. It's time to unravel the wonders of our brains and bones and to showcase the incredible tapestry of unusual talents that make each of us a marvel in our own right.

WONDERS OF THE HUMAN BODY

Hungry Tummy: Borborygmi is the noise your stomach makes when it's hungry. It's like a grumbling concert hall in your belly. Some orchestras are louder than others!

Skeleton Strength: An adult's skeleton weighs about 10 kilograms (22 pounds). That's roughly the same weight as a bicycle or a large cat!

Brain Wonders: Your brain is a hive of activity – around 100 billion nerve cells and 100 trillion connections. There are so many nerve cells that it would take almost 3,000 years to count them all. That's like counting the stars in the sky!

Mighty Femur: The femur, our biggest bone, can support 30 times your weight! That's stronger than steel. You have a super-strong pillar inside your leg.

Colour Symphony: People with chromesthesia 'see' colours when they hear sounds. Sounds pretty entertaining!

Feet's Bones: In an adult, 25% of all your bones are in your feet. It's amazing to think that they all fit into such a small body part.

Raise an Eyebrow: The average person has about 250 hairs per eyebrow, and each hair has a lifespan of about four months. Amazingly, the shape of your eyebrows can hint at your personality.

WOW

Growing Ears and Nose: Your ears and nose may look like they never stop growing as you get older. This is because they are made of cartilage which sags with gravity over the years, and the cheeks also lose volume so the ears and nose often look bigger in comparison.

Bacteria Party: Your mouth is like a city for bacteria – there are more of them than there are people in the whole world. In fact, there are ten times more bacteria in your body than human cells. And you've got about two kilograms of bacteria in your belly. They're like tiny passengers on your body's journey. A lot of them are super helpful and necessary for good health!

Sweaty Feet: Your feet have around 250,000 sweat glands and can produce about 250 millilitres (half a pint) of sweat a day. That's like a big cup full of sweat! There are more sweat glands on the feet than anywhere else on the body.

Speedy Messages: Messages from your brain travel through your nerves at speeds of up to 432 kilometres per hour (286 miles per hour)! Information races down a superhighway in your body.

SKIN SUIT

An average adult's skin may weigh around 3.6 kilograms (7.9 pounds), which is the weight of a newborn baby. It would be around two square metres if laid out flat! You get a fresh top layer, called the epidermis, every 30 days.

Thirsty Years: By the time you're 70, you'll probably have drunk over 45,000 litres (nearly 12,000 gallons) of water. That's like filling a small swimming pool!

Fingerprint Forever: No matter how damaged fingerprints get, they'll always grow back in their original pattern. It's like having a built-in identity card.

DNA Highway: If you stretched out all your DNA, it could reach from Earth to Pluto and back.

Muscle Workout: Taking just one step uses up to 200 muscles. So, every time you walk, it's a good workout for your body.

Super Pinky: Your little finger is small, but it's strong. It gives your hand 50% of its strength.

Skin Particles: Every hour, you shed about 600,000 tiny pieces of skin. In a year, that's like losing 680 grams of skin: more than a normal bread loaf.

Tongue Print: Just like fingerprints, each person has a unique tongue print. Your tongue has its own special signature.

Long Intestine: Your small intestine is super long, about three times your height!

Sneeze Speed: A sneeze can travel more than 160 kilometres per hour (100 miles per hour), which is quicker than cars are allowed to go on the highway!

Saliva Factory: In your lifetime, you'll produce 20,000 litres (5,283 gallons) of saliva. That's enough to fill 40 bathtubs!

Strong Jaw: The jaw muscle is the strongest in your body. It's a powerhouse for chewing!

Liver's Magic: The liver is a magician – it's the only organ that can completely grow back if it's damaged, even if only 25% of it is left (but don't let it get hurt too much)!

Blink Count: Your eyes blink between 14,400 and 19,200 times in just one day and around 4,200,000 times a year. When did you last blink? I bet you just did!

Food Processor: Your body processes about 45,000 kilograms (99,000 pounds) of food during your life. What a mountain of munchies!

Eating Time: We spend on average four to five years of our lives eating. That's a lot of tasty mouthfuls to look forward to.

Walking Journey: On average, a person walks about 160,000 kilometres (nearly 100,000 miles) in their lifetime, the same as walking around the Earth four times at the equator!

Blood's Journey: Your blood travels about 19,000 kilometres (11,800 miles) every day, which is further than a super wide ocean!

Heart's Beat: Your heart beats over three billion times during your life like a drum that never stops playing.

Lightbulb moment: The electrical signals zipping around between your 100 million brain cells (neurons) as they communicate with one another produce enough energy (23 watts) to power a small lightbulb! No wonder you have so many bright ideas.

Colour Wizard: Your eyes can see about 10 million different colours and of those colours, humans detect more shades of green than any other colour. Maybe that's one of the reasons we love nature so much!

Super Skeleton: Your skeleton renews itself completely every 10 years. Funnybones!

Cell City: Your body is a bustling city of cells. It's home to over 35 trillion cells, which is about 5,000 times more than the number of people on the whole planet. Imagine a massive city of tiny inhabitants.

Atomic Body: Your body is made up of about seven octillion atoms, a huge, unimaginable number! One octillion is the number one followed by 27 zeros...

The Glabella: The space between your eyebrows is called the 'glabella.'

Noisy Eyeballs: Some people can hear their eyeballs moving around in their head.

Breath Count: Every day, a person takes around 23,040 breaths. In your whole lifetime, you'll take about 673,000,000 breaths.

Skin Thickness: The skin on your feet is pretty thick, while the skin on your eyelids is incredibly thin. Think of it as a tough shield on your soles and delicate paper on your lids.

Lip Balm History: Before lip balm, people used all sorts of things to treat chapped lips, like earwax! Seems like a pretty yucky thought to us modern folk.

Finger Power: Fingers don't have their own muscles to move. Instead, they're powered by muscles in your forearm. So your arms are the puppet masters to your fingers.

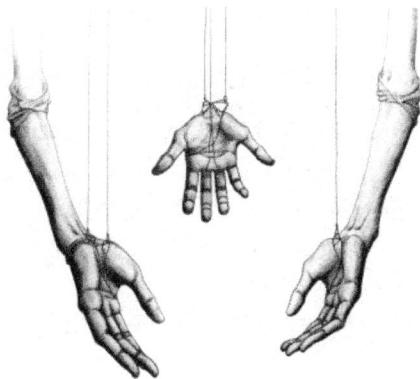

Blood Colours: Blood in arteries is bright red, and blood in veins is dark red. It's never blue, despite what you might think.

Knee Stress: For every 500 grams you weigh, your knees receive four times that amount of stress. Your knees do lots of heavy lifting!

Scalp Secrets: On average, there are about 100,000 hairs on your scalp. Hair grows about 12–15 centimetres (five to six inches) a year into a lush garden on your head!

LEFT-HANDEDNESS

Unique Lefties: Around 10-12% of people around the world are left-handed. That means if you look around a group of people, say a school class, there's probably a lefty or two!

Lefty Gene: There's this gene called LRRTM1, and it's a big deal in left-handedness, along with some other genes. And guess what? It's often passed down from dads to their kids, so being a lefty could be more common in certain families. Are there any lefties in your family?

Cultural Beliefs: Lefties have some nicknames, like 'mancinism,' 'cack handedness,' and 'southpaw.' Historically some of these names have been offensive, but these days left-handers are celebrated for the creativity they bring to the world. Different cultures have had all kinds of ideas about lefties. Some thought they had magic powers.

Twins and Lefties: Left-handedness is more common in twins than in the regular crowd. Similarly, some scientists believe that being left-handed might have something to do with having a 'Vanishing Twin' in the womb or having a twin who didn't make it.

Quick Thinkers: Lefties have a cool brain trick – they can connect the right and left sides of their brains faster than right-handers.

Lefty Guys: More men are left-handed than women, according to the latest research. But there's not a big difference between the genders.

GOOSEBUMPS

Got Goosebumps? They're like a cool link to when we were more like other animals. You know how sometimes you get tiny bumps on your skin when you're cold or scared? Well, those bumps are called goosebumps.

So, here's the deal: Underneath your skin, there are these tiny muscles that can make your hair stand up. They do this by pulling your hair upright. For animals with lots of fur, like dogs or cats, this helps them puff up their fur to keep warm or even look more intimidating.

But for us humans, who don't have much body hair, it doesn't do much for our appearance. It just makes our skin look kinda weird when those muscles tense up. So, when you shiver because it's chilly or you get spooked by something, those little muscles go into action.

Oh, and have you ever felt your hair stand on end when you're super scared or have an extra intense memory? That's the same thing happening. But now, even though we still get that funny feeling, it doesn't make us look any tougher. We're just stuck with the strange bumpy skin

✧ UNUSUAL TALENTS (wow!)

Synesthesia is like having your senses all mixed up in a cool way. Some people with synesthesia see colours when they look at numbers or letters, while others can taste things when they hear specific words. For example, imagine tasting the flavour of cherry each time you see a red brick, even though you're not tasting anything!

The brains of people with synesthesia create unexpected connections between different senses. It's most often genetic and doesn't interfere with a person's ability to function. In fact, many people with synesthesia don't even realise their experiences are different from others until later in life. Some famous people, like author Vladimir Nabokov and composer Olivier Messiaen, have synesthesia too.

THE FEARLESS LADY

A lady just known as 'SM' has a mysterious disease that caused her brain's fear control centre, called the amygdala, to completely deteriorate. Now, no matter how scary the situation, she can't feel fear at all! In a study, she watched the scariest movies and even touched a snake's tongue, but she didn't get scared. Sounds like a useful power when you have a spider in your bedroom…

Let's meet Wim Hof, also known as The Iceman. He can withstand really cold temperatures without getting cold! He once climbed Mount Everest wearing only a pair of bicycle shorts, even though it was seriously cold. Most people would have frozen within minutes, but not Wim! He now teaches his special methods to others, and he even led a group of people with serious health conditions up Mount Kilimanjaro in just shorts. They all made it, and some of them even got better!

54

Dean Karnazes is a superhuman runner! Normally, when we run for a long time, our muscles get tired because of something called lactate buildup. But not for Dean! His muscles are different. They don't get affected by the lactate buildup, so he can run forever without getting tired. When Dean was in high school, he amazed everyone by running 105 laps while his teammates could only do 15. Scientists tested him and he ran on a treadmill for over an hour when they thought he would stop in just 15 minutes! Because of his special ability, he once ran an incredible 50 marathons in 50 days. That's like running all the way down the middle of the US, from the Canadian border to the Mexican border!

An artist named Lee Hadwin has a truly extraordinary talent. But here's the twist – he only paints when he is fast asleep! Lee had always loved art, but it wasn't until he was a teenager that his unique talent appeared. Every night, when he fell into a deep sleep, something bizarre would happen. Lee would pick up a paintbrush and create beautiful paintings without even realising it. When he woke up in the morning, he would be surprised to find his artwork waiting for him, as if it had magically appeared overnight.

Now, you might be wondering, how did Lee even know he was painting in his sleep if he couldn't remember doing it? Well, his family and friends set up cameras to capture his sleep-time artistic adventures. They were amazed when they saw him paint with such skill and precision, all while his eyes were closed and he was completely unaware of what he was doing.

People from all over the world started noticing his talent and wanted to see his sleep-made masterpieces. His artwork was displayed in galleries, and people couldn't believe that someone could create such beautiful pieces without even being awake!

Rathakrishnan Velu has teeth of steel! He can pull really heavy weights, even over 200 tonnes (220 imperial tons), just using his teeth. He says that he learnt this talent when he was just 14 years old from an Indian guru who taught him how to channel all his power into one part of his body.

Supertasters are people who have an incredible sense of taste. These super-powered taste buds make them experience flavours with more intensity than the rest of us. They have extra mushroom-shaped bumps on their tongues called fungiform papillae, which are covered in taste buds. Supertasters find bitterness the most noticeable taste. Imagine having taste buds that can detect flavours so strongly! One in every four people are supertasters. Then, about a quarter of people are not as sensitive to taste, and we call them 'Non-tasters.' Can you think of anyone you know who might be one or the other?

The amazing Sherpas of Nepal and Tibet guide climbers up Mount Everest, the tallest mountain in the world! They have special traits that help them survive in the high mountains, way above sea level. Scientists discovered that 87% of Tibetans have a special gene that lets them use less oxygen than most people. It's like they have superpowers to handle the thin air up there!

Tibetan monks have a special form of meditation called 'Tum-mo' that lets them control their body temperature. When they practise Tum-mo, their fingers and toes can get 8°C (14°F) warmer! But that's not all. Through other types of meditation, these monks can lower their metabolism, which controls how fast the body breaks down calories. They can lower it by a whopping 64%, while us regular folk can only lower it by 15% when we're asleep. This means they can conserve their energy and do incredible things that others can't.

Mr Ronningsbakken is a death-defying performer. He fell in love with balancing when he was just five years old after seeing someone do amazing things on TV. When he turned 18, he joined a circus and performed there for 11 years. Ronningsbakken does mind-boggling tricks like riding a bicycle on a tightrope over a canyon and doing handstands on a bar hanging under a flying hot-air balloon. He even rode a bicycle backwards down one of the curviest roads in Norway! Mr Ronningsbakken admits he gets anxious before some stunts, but that's what makes him human and keeps him going. If he ever lost his fear, he'd quit because he believes it's an important part of being fully human.

Some people have 'perfect pitch', the amazing ability to identify and reproduce a tone without any reference. They can name a note just by hearing it, recognize the tones in a chord, or even name the key signature of a song. This talent requires remembering the frequencies of different tones and having exposure to a wide range of sounds. Estimates show that about 3% to 8% of the general population have this amazing ability, and it's even more common among musicians. In fact, in music conservatories in Japan, a whopping 70% of musicians have perfect pitch.

Tetrachromacy is like having super-powered vision. Most humans are trichromats, which means they have three types of cone cells in their eyes to see different colours. But tetrachromats have an extra type of cone, allowing them to see light from four distinct sources. True tetrachromacy is quite rare in humans, but it's more common in women. They might be able to perceive a whopping 100 million colours! (That's 100 times more than the rest of us.)

Daniel Browning Smith is known as the most flexible man alive. He can bend and twist his body in incredible ways. He can even dislocate his arms to fit his whole body through an unstrung tennis racket! That's why people call him the 'rubber boy.'

Michel Lotito is a French man known as 'Monsieur Mangetout' or 'Mr. Eat it All.' This guy can eat anything! He can swallow metal, rubber, and things that normal people can't even imagine eating. His stomach is made of tough stuff!

In Scotland, there is a lady named Jo who can't feel any pain. It wasn't until she went to the hospital for an operation on her hand that they discovered her unique condition. Scientists at a hospital in London did some tests and found out that her body had a lot of something called anandamide. That's why she couldn't feel pain, anxiety, or fear. But even though she couldn't feel any pain herself, she was kind and wanted to help others. So, she decided to work with scientists to find the gene that caused her condition. They wanted to create natural pain relief for people without using drugs that could be addictive. They got the money to do more research, and since she shared her story, 80 people from around the world have come forward, thinking they have a similar condition.

Echolocation is a skill that some blind people use to 'see' their surroundings. It's a similar process to how bats navigate! They make sounds, like clicking their tongue or tapping a cane, and then listen for the echoes that bounce back. By interpreting the echoes, they can figure out where objects are and how far away they are. It's an incredible way to navigate and understand the environment without using their eyes. People who have mastered echolocation, like James Holman, Daniel Kish, and Ben Underwood, have shown us just how amazing this ability can be.

A condition called 'genetic chimerism' is like being your own twin! It happens when two fertilised eggs or embryos fuse together in the early stages of pregnancy. Each cell keeps its own genetic identity, so the resulting person becomes a mixture of two sets of DNA. It's super rare, with only about 40 reported cases ever.

$$x = \frac{-b \pm \sqrt{b^2 - 4ac}}{2a}$$

$$y = mx + b$$

Mental calculators are people who can do super fast maths in their heads. Some of the most amazing mental calculators are autistic savants, who have a special gift for numbers. They can solve complex calculations without using a calculator or pen and paper! Their brains work in a unique way, allowing them to process maths much faster than the average person.

Eidetic memory, also known as photographic memory, is like having a camera in your brain that captures everything you see and remembers it with incredible detail. Imagine being able to recall sounds, images, or objects from your memory with extreme accuracy. Some people with eidetic memory can even remember thousands of books word for word!

A boy named Derek Paravicini was born blind but he had an incredible musical talent! When he was just a little baby, his nanny gave him a toy organ to play with. To everyone's surprise, he was able to play music he had heard all by himself, without any help. As Derek's talent grew he could play any song people asked for, as long as he had heard it before. Derek has performed in many different places, sharing his musical ability with people around the world.

Prahlad Jani is a man who claims he can survive without food and water. He says he hasn't eaten anything since way back in 1940! That's a looong time ago! Now, you're probably wondering how he manages to stay alive without food and water, right? Scientists did an experiment and kept him in a room for 10 days and watched him closely. They found that Prahlad Jani was perfectly healthy even without eating or drinking anything! We're still waiting for the scientific explanation for this one.

STRANGE THINGS OUR BODIES CAN DO

The Scent of Time Travel: Ever smelled something that brought memories flooding back? That's because your sense of smell is highly connected to your memories and feelings. When you smell something familiar, it's like mentally travelling back in time.

Forecasting Joints: You might have heard about people saying they can predict rain because their joints hurt. Well, it's not just a story. When a big storm is on the way, the air pressure changes and it can make people's joints, like hips and knees, feel more painful. So, those folks who seem to 'know' it's going to rain might just be listening to their bodies!

PSYCHIC HEARTS

Your heart can't tell the future like a crystal ball, but it can be a bit of a fortune-teller sometimes. Scientists have noticed that it actually starts to speed up *before* something exciting or surprising happens. It's like your heart can sense when things are about to get interesting.

Pupils as a Clue: If you want to keep your feelings a secret, stay in low light when that special someone is around. Your eyes might give you away because when you're attracted to someone, your pupils get bigger. It's like a little hint from your eyes that you really like someone.

Spring Alert: Even before spring arrives, your eyes can tell you it's coming. As plants start releasing pollen and stuff, your eyes might get itchy and watery. It's like your eyes saying, 'Hey, spring is on its way!'

Digestive System Standby: When you're in real danger, your body can do some incredible things. Your body releases a hormone called adrenaline, which makes your heart race, your pupils get bigger and even slows down your digestion. All this is to give your muscles extra energy, so you can be super strong when you truly need it.

Snow Blind: Here's another energy-saver. When you're really, really cold, your eyes start to show signs. The blood vessels in your eyes get smaller to save energy, and sometimes, this can even make you temporarily blind.

AMAZING HEIGHTS

Tallest Human in History: Imagine giants walking among us! The tallest verified humans in history were truly extraordinary. Robert Wadlow, known as the 'Alton Giant,' holds the record for the tallest person ever recorded. He lived between 1918 and 1940 and was a towering 2.7 metres (8 feet 11 inches) tall!

Tallest Living Humans: Whoa, there are some seriously tall people walking around today too! The current tallest living person is Sultan Kösen from Turkey. He stands at a remarkable height of 2.5 metres (8 feet 2.8 inches). The ceilings in many homes aren't that high… the world is not adapted for people as tall as Sultan!

AFTER DARK

Let's embark on a journey that starts when the lights go out! In this chapter, we explore the wonders of sleep and the enchanting realm of dreams. We'll unveil the incredible ways in which these nocturnal adventures have inspired people and changed the course of history.

SLEEP

Sleep Avoiders: We humans are the only mammals who choose to stay up late even when we're tired. We're the kings and queens of bedtime procrastination!

Sleep vs. Food: Surprisingly, going without sleep can be more dangerous than going without food. Make sure you get your twenty winks.

Moon Mysteries: People tend to sleep less and stay up later when there's a full moon, but no one knows exactly why!

Insomnia Invaders: Lots of things can mess with our sleep, like stress, illness, or even what we eat. Sometimes, it can be a bit puzzling to work out why you can't fall asleep.

Whale Brain Balance: Whales and dolphins are super smart sleepers. They let one side of their brain nap while the other side stays awake. It's like they take turns getting rest and staying alert.

Sleepy Creatures: Giraffes need less sleep than us, only about 1.9 hours a day! Humans spend about a third of their lives asleep. Cats take it to the next level, sleeping for about two-thirds of their lives. But brown bats are the champs, snoozing for almost 20 hours.

Pain and Sleep: Lack of sleep can make you more sensitive to pain because your body's defence system gets a bit wonky without enough rest.

Sleepless Record: Can you believe someone stayed awake for 11 whole days? That's a superhuman feat of sleeplessness!

The Dead Zone: Our natural body clocks means that if we stay awake all night, we will feel more tired at 4am than at 10am. The period from 3am to 5am is the 'dead zone' when our body clock makes us 'dead' tired.

Sleep Positions: Believe it or not, your sleeping position can say something about your personality! For example, people who naturally sleep on their stomachs with their heads turned may be more confident and bold.

UP TO 15% OF PEOPLE MAY SLEEPWALK

Money and Sleep: People who earn more money tend to sleep better. It makes a lot of sense knowing that stress can disturb sleep.

Monday Morning: Waking up on Mondays can be extra tough because our sleep patterns change over the weekend.

Morning Struggle: Having a tough time getting out of bed in the morning? It's a real thing called dysania.

Speedy Sleep: If you fall asleep in less than five minutes, you might not be getting enough sleep. Ideally, it should take you about 10 to 15 minutes to drift off peacefully.

DREAMS

Dreaming in Colour: Scientists have found that people under 25 almost never dream in black and white, but one in four people over the age of 55 sometimes do. How strange!

Dreaming Blind: People born blind dream with their other senses, like sounds and smells. Amazing.

What you eat can even affect your dreams. Foods rich in vitamin B6, like bananas and spinach, can make your dreams more vivid and exciting, so keep eating those healthy snacks.

Falling Dreams: Ever felt like you're falling and suddenly woke up? That's called 'hypnic jerks.' It's like your body's way of saying, 'Oops, not yet!'

Some dreams are common all around the world even in different cultures. People often dream about flying, being chased, or even being unable to move. Do you dream about the same things as the people you know?

Everybody dreams, even if you can't remember them. When we're in a special sleep called REM, our brain gets super active and we have the most vivid dreams.

Lucid dreaming is when you know you're dreaming. It's like being the boss of your dream world! Anyone can learn to control their dreams with consistency, patience, and ambition. Cool!

Our brains are extra active while we dream. They're busy processing information, learning from the day, and making sense of everything we've experienced. Who knew we had a brain workout every night?

Dream Memory: Within five minutes of waking up, we forget about half of our dreams. So, if you want to remember your dreams, jot them down right away!

Dreams can be super creative. They can inspire artists, problem solvers, and anyone who loves to use their imagination. You might get awesome ideas from your dreams that you can use in your everyday life.

DREAMS THAT CHANGED HISTORY

Theory of Relativity: Albert Einstein, the famous scientist, once had a dream about cows. In his dream, he saw cows jumping at the same time when they got an electric shock from a fence. But a farmer on the other side of the field saw them jumping one by one, like a wave at a game. Einstein realised that how we see things can be different depending on where we're standing because it takes time for light to reach our eyes. This idea became his world-changing Theory of Relativity. Imagine if he hadn't remembered that dream!

Inception: Seen that mind-bending movie? Well, it was inspired by a series of lucid dreams that the director, Chris Nolan, had. He turned those dreams into an epic movie that made us question reality!

Google: Yup, even the famous Google search engine started with a dream. Larry Page had this fear that he'd be kicked out of college, and that sparked a dream of downloading the whole internet onto PCs. That dream turned into the searchable Google we know today.

The Shape of DNA: Dr James Watson had some wild dreams that helped him understand the structure of DNA. In one dream, he saw a double-sided staircase, and in another, two snakes coiled around each other. Those dreams unravelled the secrets of one of the most important discoveries of our time.

The Periodic Table of Elements: Imagine seeing all the elements of the periodic table fall into place on a table. That's exactly what happened to Dmitri Mendeleev in a dream! His dream made it easy to organise all those elements and created the periodic table we use today.

The Sewing Machine: Imagine this – Elias Howe, the creator of the sewing machine, had a dream where cannibals threatened him! They wanted a design for the sewing machine, or else! Talk about a dream with a stitch of danger.

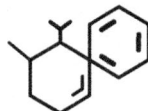

Structure of Benzene: In the 1800s, August Kekulé was trying to figure out how atoms in benzene fit together. He was mulling over these tricky carbon and hydrogen puzzles but he couldn't crack the code, so he decided to take a nap by the fire. And guess what he dreamed about? Atoms having a little dance party! They formed a snake that ended up biting its own tail. This was his "Aha!" moment. The snake dream was a clue – benzene molecules are like rings of carbon atoms. That discovery opened up a whole new chapter in chemistry called aromatic chemistry.

Mega Maths: Srinivasa Ramanujan, was an incredible maths whiz with very little formal training. Sadly, he passed away at 32, but he left behind a treasure trove of over 4,000 maths nuggets, and in the 1920s many of his ideas were ahead of their time. Ramanujan claimed a Hindu goddess named Namagiri visited his dreams, dropping mathematical wisdom. One time, he dreamt of a red screen made of flowing blood (a bit intense, right?), and a mystical hand started scribbling elliptic integrals.

HABIT
RABBIT

GET IN THE

HABIT

Habits and daily routines can sound a bit dull, right? But remember, our days are basically a collection of habits, so tweaking them is like turning up the enjoyment level in life from 'Average' or 'Good' to 'Outstanding'.

Being active is a big deal for staying healthy. Think about those superathletes you see on TV. They have a tiny chance of getting seriously sick. But, not moving around is like doing something really bad for your body, like smoking or eating too much candy.

You can do this thing called meditation, which is like a mini-vacation for your mind. Researchers in the Netherlands found that regularly meditating is like going on a week-long vacation, but better because it keeps making you feel good even after a really long time. Even 10 minutes a day can be a gamechanger.

Remember to look on the bright side of a situation. If you're thankful for stuff, you can feel happier, less stressed, and even healthier! Why not start by writing down things you're thankful for? As French writer Alphonse Karr said, 'We can complain about thorny roses or be happy that thorns have roses.'

Ever heard that saying, 'You are who your friends are'? Well, it's kinda true! Hang out with folks who make you feel awesome because happiness is catchy. When you're with happy people, they sprinkle happiness on you, and suddenly, life feels more amazing!

Exercise isn't just about being strong; it's also like a booster for your brain. It gives you more bright ideas, lots of energy, and makes you super happy. It's because your brain makes these feel-good things called endorphins when you move around.

You know how laughing makes you feel awesome, right? Well, guess what? A bunch of scientists found out that old folks who giggle every day have way less chance of heart problems.

Listening to others is super important for making friends and keeping them. If you listen really well when people talk you understand them better, and that makes your friendships extra strong. So, listen up and care about what others say!

HABITS OF THE FAMOUS

Being famous certainly isn't all fun and games, but what do most famous people have in common? Motivation and determination! They became a big name because they got back up after every fall. That makes celebrities a good group to turn to for habits to help you achieve your goals… or wildest dreams!

Write: You know what quite a few famous artists, singers and writers do when they wake up? They scribble down three pages of whatever's dancing around in their heads. No need to be neat or fancy, just let it all out! It's like tidying up your brain, making it super sharp and ready to think up amazing stuff.

MIND CONTROL

Meditate: Oprah Winfrey starts her day with something peaceful. She sits quietly for 20 minutes, clears away her busy thoughts and focuses on just one thing, like her breathing. It's like giving your brain a gentle massage. This helps you focus, stay calm, and stay strong against germs, and it's great for your mood too!

Question: Ever wondered what smart folks like Steve Jobs and Benjamin Franklin did in the morning? They asked themselves some pretty important questions. Like, Steve asked, 'If today was my last day, would I want to do what I'm doing now?' And Benjamin asked, 'What good can I do today?' The questions keep you super motivated to do good and chase your dreams.

BENEFITS OF HUGGING

... IN CASE YOU NEEDED ANOTHER REASON FOR A GOOD CUDDLE.

Happy Hormone: After hugging for about 20 seconds, your body releases a special hormone called oxytocin. It's like a dose of happiness and is responsible for that warm, fuzzy feeling during a hug.

Pain Relief: Just like how oxytocin is released to help with pain during childbirth, hugging for over 20 seconds can also make pain feel a bit better.

Stress Buster: Hugging can make you feel super relaxed and calm, helping you deal with stress, worry, and feeling down.

Fight Off Germs: Regular hugs are a secret to staying healthy. They help your body fight off sickness by getting your hormones in balance and giving your immune system a boost.

Happy Heart: When you hug someone tight, your blood pressure can drop, and that's a good thing. It's like giving your heart a break and keeping it strong.

Bonding Time: Hugging makes your connections with people even stronger. It's a way to say, 'I trust you, and I care about you a lot.'

Sleep Tight: Hugging helps you relax and get ready for a good night's sleep. It tells your body, 'Time to rest and have sweet dreams.'

BLUE ZONES

Blue zones are special places around the world where people live incredibly long and healthy lives. In these unique areas, like Ikaria in Greece, Okinawa in Japan, Sardinia in Italy, Loma Linda in California, and the Nicoya Peninsula in Costa Rica, folks have secrets to their longevity. They keep moving by doing everyday tasks and eat wholesome foods with an emphasis on plants. Strong communities and a sense of purpose are common, and they share a commitment to staying healthy. These practices help them live longer, happier lives, and each blue zone has its unique way of doing it, but here are some of the main things that we've learned...

Eat Mindfully: Sometimes, food tastes so good that we eat too much. In the blue zones, they follow a rule – they stop eating when they're about 80% full. They also eat their biggest meal early in the day and a smaller one later on, which helps them sleep better and stay at a healthy weight.

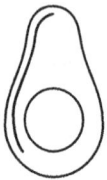

Go Plant-Based: Most of the food in these special places comes from plants like beans, tofu, and miso. They do eat meat sometimes, but only in small amounts. Their diet is full of yummy plant-based stuff, and that keeps them healthy.

Enjoy Alcohol in Moderation: Some of these super long-living folks have a drink or two, but not too much. Studies show that if they do drink it's only to have a glass with their meals or friends, and it's a fun tradition.

FIND YOUR PURPOSE

People in some special places called 'blue zones', have this strong reason for waking up in the morning. It's not just about work; it's about having a big goal that makes life exciting. Having a purpose can make you stronger, happier, and even live longer – like seven years longer!

Stress Less: We all know stress can be a real pain. Even in the blue zones, people have their own tricks to handle stress. Some of them have a daily catch-up with friends, while others take a little nap in the afternoon to relax. It's their way of staying cool and living longer.

● ● ● ● ● ● ● ● ● ● ● ● ●

Natural Movement: You know how people often go to the gym or run to stay healthy? Well, the folks who live the longest don't really do that. They keep moving by walking, taking care of their gardens, and cooking their meals from scratch. It's like exercise without even trying!

Build a Community: Being part of a group where you share beliefs is something many of these long-living people do. They go to their community gatherings regularly, which can add four years to their lives! It doesn't matter which religion or group you're in; it's all about being together.

Family Matters: Family is a big deal in these special places. People there stick with their life partners and take care of their older family members. It's like an exchange of love and support, and it keeps everyone strong and happy.

Find Your Tribe: You've probably heard that your friends can influence you. Well, it's true! In the blue zones, they stick with friends who help them stay healthy. They even create groups to support each other emotionally and financially when needed.

● ● ● ● ● ● ● ● ● ● ● ● ●

THE WAY
WE LIVE

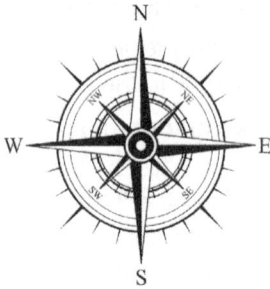

Humans are a pretty diverse bunch of creatures. Delve into the quirks of daily life with bizarre laws, the best April Fool's jokes, and timeless wisdom from around the world.

STRANGE LAWS

Sometimes laws take a while to catch up with the modern world. Here are some that were created to deal with problems in the olden days, but now seem strange and often absurd! Thankfully, the police don't take the silliest ones too seriously, either.

Texas: Need cash? Selling your eye won't help. Plus, it's against the law.

Devon, Texas: DIY furniture makers, beware! Crafting tables and chairs in the nude could land you in trouble.

Spain: Building sandcastles is illegal in some parts, and if caught, you could be fined. Not even kids are exempt; their parents have to pay.

Baltimore, Maryland: Inviting your lion out? Not in Baltimore! Taking a lion to the cinema is banned.

Oklahoma: Beware of the hounds! Making ugly faces at a dog can get you arrested.

Samoa: Got a great memory? Good, because forgetting your wife's birthday is a crime here.

Miami, Florida: Skateboarding fun? Not inside a police station.

Louisiana: Biting someone with your natural teeth is 'simple' assault, but with dentures, it's 'aggravated'!

Victoria, Australia: Light bulb out? You'll need a licensed electrician to fix it.

British Parliament: Had you planned on wearing your suit of armour today? Stay out of the British Parliament buildings. It's illegal there.

Poland: Winnie the Pooh is banned around playgrounds and schools due to concerns about the character's lack of pants.

San Francisco: Horse manure pile-up alert! You better not stack it more than six feet high on street corners, or you might face the consequences.

Kentucky: Ice cream lovers, don't put cones in your pockets! It's breaking the rules!

California: Ready for a wild ride? Well, don't let your driverless vehicle go above 60 miles per hour (97 kilometres per hour). That's a no-no.

South Dakota: It's illegal to sleep in a cheese factory – so stay awake and munch some Camembert.

France: Men are required by law to wear Speedos on beaches and public swimming areas, ensuring that swimsuits are clean and not worn all day.

China: Tibetan Buddhist monks cannot reincarnate without government permission after they die. It's an unusual law that is impossible to enforce.

United Arab Emirates (UAE): Parents told you not to curse? You'd better listen to them if you're in the UAE, where it can lead to fines, jail time, or deportation.

Miami, Florida: No monkey business allowed. Imitating animals in Miami is illegal.

Singapore: No chewing! But not just in class. Gum is totally illegal everywhere in Singapore.

Russia: Better get down to the carwash. Driving a dirty car is illegal.

Oklahoma: Bathing your donkey at bedtime? Not after 7pm.

Illinois: Pets don't need cigars! Giving a lit one to your furry friend is outlawed here and probably every other place in the world.

Alabama: Blindfolded driving? Not a great idea. And what a surprise. It's illegal!

Tennessee: Falling asleep at the wheel? It's not just dangerous; it's against the law. Stay awake, folks!

Ohio: Keep fish sober. No booze for them while you're fishing.

Providence, Rhode Island: You mean you want me to sell you a toothbrush and a tube of toothpaste? On a Sunday? Outrageous. And fully illegal.

San Francisco, California: Car wash caution. Cleaning the car with used knickers could do more than embarrass your family.

Chico, California: Nuclear blasts not allowed. Detonate one and face a hefty… fine.

London, England: City cabs have strict policies – no rabid dogs or corpses allowed on board! And don't even think of hailing a cab if you're suffering from the plague.

Kentucky: This one must be hard to stick to. Keep your lawn green, not red. Painting it red is breaking the law.

Chicago: Need a hot dinner? Eating in a burning place is illegal.

Iowa: Seems fire hydrants are popular fodder for very specific laws. Horses can't munch on fire hydrants here!

Salt Lake County, Utah: Keep your violin out of paper bags when strolling down the street. It's against the law. Who knows why?

Australia: Give names wisely. Naming an animal you plan to eat is illegal Down Under!

England: Heads up, folks. Dying inside the Houses of Parliament is strictly forbidden.

Sweden: Until earlier this year, dancing in bars or lounges without a dancing licence was against the law and was strictly enforced.

Arizona: Camel hunters, think twice. Firstly, because hunting these desert animals is against the law. Secondly, because there aren't any wild camels in Arizona.

British Columbia: Watch out for Sasquatch! It's illegal to harm Bigfoot.

TOP APRIL FOOLS JOKES

GOTCHA!

Smell-O-Vision: The BBC in 1965 said they had a smell TV! People thought it was real and reported smelling things from TV shows.

Lion-Washing Prank: The earliest April Fools' joke recorded was way back in 1689. They made fake tickets for the fake lion-washing ceremony at the Tower of London that didn't exist. Lots of people showed up and got tricked, and it became a funny tradition.

π

Pi Prank: In 1998, they said Alabama would change the number pi to exactly three. People got upset until they found out it was just a joke.

Bunny Birth: In 1726, a woman named Mary Toft claimed she gave birth to animal parts and bunnies! People were amazed until they found out it was all a trick with real rabbits.

War of the Worlds: In 1938, a radio show made it sound like aliens were invading. People panicked, thinking it was real. It's one of the most famous hoaxes ever.

Treasury Tunnel: In 1905, a newspaper said thieves stole all US gold by digging tunnels. Everyone freaked out, but it was all fake news!

Dino Invasion: In 1906, newspapers said dinosaurs invaded Chicago. They even showed fake pictures of dinos in the city.

Metric Time: On Australian TV in 1975, there was a big hoax that said the country would be converting to 'metric time,' which meant 100 seconds in every minute, 100 minutes in an hour, and 20 hours in a day!

Big Ben Beeps: In 1980, the BBC said the chimes of Big Ben's famous clock would become digital beeps. Some folks believed it and got mad!

Spaghetti Trees: In 1957, the BBC news programme said spaghetti grew on trees in Switzerland. People believed it and asked how to grow their own. The reply: 'Put spaghetti in tomato sauce and hope!'

Rhinoceros Councilor: In 1956, a rhino named 'Cacareco' won a city council seat in Brazil! Students were tired of bad city management. This one wasn't a joke!

HANS THE CLEVER HORSE

A horse named Hans seemed super smart, doing maths and reading German in the 1900s. But he was just following his owner's signals without anyone knowing it!

Animal Antics: In 2016, National Geographic joked they'd show dressed-up puppies and kittens because they didn't want to show naked animals anymore.

Threenie Money: In 2008, they joked Canada would have a three-dollar coin called a 'threenie.'

Fairy Tale: In 2007, a magician's website had pictures of a 'mummified fairy.' Lots of folks believed in fairies for a while!

Loch Ness Monster: The Loch Ness monster legend began in 1933 with a fake sighting. Even a doctor's photos fooled people for years, but it turned out to be a toy submarine.

Moon Fantasy: In 1835, a newspaper claimed there were people, unicorns, and winged humans living on the moon. People believed it, preferring a world of magic over reality.

Tree Octopus Trick: Online, there's a story about a tree-dwelling octopus in Washington State. It's all fake, but even some older kids fell for it. Remember, not everything on the internet is true!

Floating Earth: In 1976, an astronomer said the planets would align, making it possible to float at exactly 9:47 am. People actually jumped in the air to see if it worked!

LIVELY LANGUAGES

HERE'S A RIDDLE FOR YOU...

I am a key to connection, a bridge of understanding,
Without me, words are mere sounds, in chaos they are landing.

In letters and in symbols, my essence lies,
I can make you laugh or cry, with the power to mesmerise.

Across borders and cultures, I effortlessly dance,
Unlocking the secrets of expression, giving life a chance.

What am I?

Answer on page 233!

E is Queen: Have you noticed that the letter 'E' is everywhere in English? It's in about 11% of all words, making it the most popular letter. 'A' is a close second.

English Around the World: More people across the globe learn English as a second language than there are folks who speak it as their first language. That's a lot of English learners!

Whistle Talk: Imagine having a secret whistling language! Some people in faraway places use whistling to talk over big mountains because regular words can't go that far. They change the shape of their mouths, the sound's pitch, and how fast or slow they whistle to say words. Like in La Gomera, a mountainous island in Spain. Similarly, in Botswana, there's a language that sounds like a symphony of clicks. It's like speaking in Morse Code.

Funny Words: English has some quirky words like 'glasses,' 'scissors,' 'jeans,' and 'pyjamas' that only exist in their plural form. Imagine having one 'jean' instead of two!

Letter Crunch: Did you know not all languages use the same number of letters? Rotokas, an indigenous language in Papua New Guinea, is the smallest known language in the world with a total of 12 letters! But then there's Cambodian (or Khmer), which has a whopping 74 letters in its alphabet. Imagine singing the alphabet song for that one!

So Many Languages: There are over 7,000 languages spoken worldwide, and most of them are like cousins or siblings of each other because they're related to the same 'parent' or 'grandparent' languages.

HOLA!

Translating Machines: The Bible has been translated into more languages than any other book. Pinocchio comes close in second place!

Alphabet Origins: The word 'alphabet' comes from the first two letters of the Greek alphabet – alpha and beta. It's like calling it the 'AB'.

Vanishing Languages: Sadly, about 2,400 languages are in danger of disappearing forever, with one language vanishing every two weeks. We should cherish our languages!

Sign Talk: Sign languages are super cool because you can say lots of things all at once! Instead of just using words, people use their hands, faces, and bodies to chat. It's like telling a story with your whole body! Even more interesting is that different countries have their unique versions of it.

你好

German Print: The first book ever printed was in German. It's like the great-great-grandparent of all printed books!

Made-Up Languages: Have you heard of Klingon from Star Trek? Well, there are more than 200 made-up languages in books, movies, and TV shows. Some people even decide to learn them, like a secret code!

Global Languages: Believe it or not, only 23 languages are spoken by more than half of the world's population. That's not a lot out of the 7,000+ global languages!

CRYPTIC COLOUR CODES

In English, we have 11 basic words for colours: black, white, red, green, yellow, blue, brown, orange, pink, purple, and grey. In Pirahã, the language of a Brazilian tribe, there are no words at all for colours, except 'dark' and 'light'! In some languages, they might use the same words for green and yellow, or pink and red, as they do not consider them to be separate colours. However, some languages have colour words that we don't have in English at all. In Russian, there are different words for light blue and dark blue, as they are considered totally different colours!

Asian and African Diversity: Most of the world's languages exist in Asia and Africa – about two-thirds of rare languages are found there.

Bilingual Superstars: At least half of the world's people can speak two languages.

Language Birth: Some super-smart folks think language started around 100,000 BC. That's so long ago that most historians don't know what was happening at that time!

Tea Talk: The way we chat about our favourite hot drink, chai or tea, depends on who we met in history. 'Chai' comes from places like China, Russia, and Arabic-speaking lands where they have similar words for it. But 'tea' started in China and travelled around other continents. That's why we have lots of similar names like 'thé,' 'té,' and 'Tee' for this tasty drink!

Unrelated Language: Basque, spoken in an area between France and Spain, is a language rebel. It's unrelated to any other known language on Earth. Where did it come from?

Word Mystery: Even though languages have tons of words, people usually use a small percentage of these in everyday conversation. Knowing the most common 3000 words of a language, even if it has more than ten times that many words in total, could make you pretty fluent.

South African Chatter: South Africa has the most official languages – 11 in total!

French in Africa: The city of Kinshasa in the Congo is the second-largest French-speaking city in the world, right after Paris.

BONJOUR!

Italian Journey: The Italian language jumped from a regional dialect to become the national language of Italy. Unlike most languages that evolve naturally, this dialect was actively chosen because it was believed to be the most bella.

European Babble: Europe is a language playground with around 24 official languages.

French Connection: French is the only language, besides English, taught in every country. It's like the world's second universal language.

Number Puzzles: Counting isn't the same in every language. While some use tens or twenties, others do it in really different ways. In Oksapmin, a place in Papua New Guinea, they use 27 as their counting base. Each number is linked to a body part, making it an interesting counting game!

German's Gender Game: German words can be picky as they have three genders: masculine, feminine, and neuter. Most languages make do with two!

German Club: German is the boss in Europe, being the most widely spoken language with four countries naming it as their official language

No Official Language: In the US, there isn't an official language, but English is the main player in most conversations.

MULTILINGUAL LONDON

London is a real melting pot of languages, with over 300 of them being spoken. You can find a new language buddy on every corner!

Korean Separation: North and South Korea have been separated for a long time, so their languages have taken different paths with unique words and grammar.

Papua New Guinea's Tongue Twister: Papua New Guinea is like a language festival, boasting a whopping 840 languages!

Spanish Warmth: When people speak Spanish, it's normal to have some friendly physical contact during a conversation.

Spanish Flavours: Spanish has a fun twist with about 4,000 Arabic words mixed in.

French Influence: Nearly 30% of English words are borrowed from French. In fact, French adds a pinch of flavour to culinary and ballet terms worldwide. Bon appétit and bravo, dancers!

Italian in Brazil: Even though Portuguese is the star language in Brazil, Italian has its own little fan club as a minority language there.

Wordy English: English holds the record for having the most words – over 250,000! We love our words!

ALOHA

Mandarin Tops the Charts: Mandarin Chinese is the world's most spoken language, allowing you to chat with over 12% of the world's people. That's a lot of conversation partners.

Hawaiian Rain Words: Hawaiians are rain experts with over 200 words for 'rain.' Imagine having a special word for every type of raindrop!

Indonesian confusion: The word 'air' means 'water' in Indonesia. Pretty confusing for English-speaking travellers. Would you like a glass of 'air' with your meal, ma'am?

Tricky 'TH' Sound: English has a sneaky sound that other languages don't always have. It's the 'th' sound, like in 'Thanks.' Some folks from other places find it puzzling because they don't have it in their language. In London, they even swap it for sounds like 'f' or 't' sometimes. 'Fanks, mate!'

Twin Language: Some twins have a special language called cryptophasia that only they can understand. It's like a secret twin code.

Japanese's Triple Play: Japanese uses three different writing styles: Kanji, Katakana, and Hiragana. There must be a lot of language classes at school!

Brain Power: People who speak Chinese use both sides of their brains, while English speakers mainly use the left side. What a brain workout!

Spanish Chat: Spanish is the world's second most spoken language. It's the official language in 20 countries, making it a great language for travellers. You can chat in Spanish all over the place! After Mexico, the US has the most Spanish speakers. ¡Hola, amigos!

REALLY SILLY LAWSUITS

Here are some of the most ridiculous things people have tried to claim money for. Thankfully, almost all failed. Enjoy reading this parade of silliness! You'll be laughing by the end of it... but don't sue me if you're not.

Emile Ratelband, a man from the Netherlands, tried to legally change his age in 2018 because he thought it would help him get better job opportunities and matches on dating sites. But the judge said no, because your age affects a lot of things, and if everyone started changing their age it would create huge problems!

A teenager found out in 2013 that his Subway 'footlong' sandwich was only 11 inches long! He sued Subway in 2016, but in the end, the lawyers were the ones who profited from it as the teenager didn't win.

In 1996, a woman in Israel sued a weatherman because he got the forecast wrong, and she got wet in the rain and caught the flu. Unexpectedly, the TV station paid her $1,000 US dollars in an out-of-court agreement, and the weatherman apologised.

Imagine suing someone for texting too much during a movie! In 2017, a guy from Texas did just that. He took his movie date to court because she was always on her phone during 'Guardians Of The Galaxy Vol. 2.' She offered to pay for her ticket, so he dropped the case.

A man sued basketball legend Michael Jordan and Nike for a combined $832 million US dollars in 2006, saying that Michael Jordan looked too much like him, and it hurt his feelings when strangers thought he was Michael Jordan. The lawsuit was dismissed by the court.

In 2007, a customer sued a dry cleaner for $54 million US dollars because they lost his trousers. He thought their 'Satisfaction Guaranteed' sign meant they had to pay him. The court said he was wrong and told him to pay their legal fees.

In 2018, three people sued the makers of Junior Mints, saying there was too much empty space in the boxes. They thought it was a trick, but the judge said most people know there might be some empty space in a box, so the case was dismissed.

In 2009, a guy kidnapped a couple, but they escaped. Then, the couple sued him! But he turned around and sued them, saying they promised to hide him from the police. The case didn't go anywhere in the end. How absurd!

Red Bull had a problem in 2016. People said their slogan, 'Red Bull gives you wings,' wasn't true because it didn't make them feel more focused or give them actual wings. Red Bull paid some money to settle the case. Unbelievable.

In 2018, two people in Florida sued McDonald's because they were charged the same price for a Quarter Pounder with or without cheese, even though there was only a small price difference. The judge said they didn't show how they were harmed, so the case was over.

In 2015, a lady in New York said she fell on the stairs at a subway station because of a scary poster for the TV show 'Dexter.' She thought it was too scary, but the judge said it wasn't the network's fault.

In 1995, a guy in prison tried to sue himself for $5 million US dollars, saying he broke his own religious rules and got himself arrested. He wanted the state to pay him because he had no income in jail. Obviously, the judge said no way.

A 15-year-old boy in Spain took his mum to court in 2007 because she took his mobile phone away to get him to study more. He wanted her to go to jail and pay for his legal costs, but the judge said she did the right thing. Can it get any sillier?

In 2016, someone tried to sue Starbucks for putting too much ice in their cold drinks, which meant you got less liquid. But the judge said everyone knows ice takes up space in a cup...

A French businessman sued Uber for $48 million US dollars in 2017, saying their app messed up his marriage because it kept sending notifications to his wife's phone.

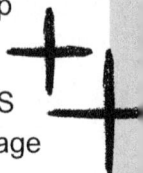

A student thought he deserved a better grade in 2003, so he sued the school to change it. He got his grade raised to a B, but the case was dismissed and he didn't get any money. Sometimes you just have to accept the grade you get!

Two teenagers were trespassing on a railway property in 2002, and they got badly hurt. But the property owners had to pay them $24.2 million US dollars even though they were trespassing!

The mayor of the city Batman, Turkey, filed a lawsuit because he didn't like how the city's name was used in 'The Dark Knight' movie in 2008. He said it hurt the city's business, but it never went to court.

UNCONTACTED TRIBES

JUNGLE MYSTERIES

Deep in remote areas like the Amazon rainforest and New Guinea there are more than 100 tribes that have never met people from the outside world. They often live in ways that have hardly changed for thousands of years. It's a big mystery how many of them there are because they keep to themselves and exploring these places is tough because of the wild terrain. Sometimes, scientists find them and try to find out some things about them, but it's not easy, and the meetings are not long enough to gather much information. Outsiders can bring threats like diseases the tribes haven't encountered before, so even things like a common cold can be deadly for them. There are also problems with some companies not respecting these tribes' lands and wrecking their environments while they steal resources to sell, like illegal logging. It's often best to respect these tribes' rights to live in peace in their ancient ways.

Ishi's Brave Story: In 1911, a guy named Ishi came out of the California forest, and he was the last surviving person from his tribe, the Yahia. He told people about how his tribe lived and survived in the wild. He had a wealth of ancient knowledge and a fascinating window into the past.

Mysterious Peruvian Encounter: Some tourists got a big surprise in the jungles of Peru when they met a tribe that no one had ever seen before. They managed to capture the meeting on camera, and even the scientists had no idea this tribe existed!

Brazil's Amazon Secrets: In the Brazilian part of the Amazon, there are tribes that we don't know much about. Sometimes, research aeroplanes are surprised when they see humans in areas where it was thought no humans have ever lived! The tribes are equally surprised by the planes and sometimes get a bit angry!

Surma People's Unique Style: In Ethiopia, there's a group called the Surma people. They love wearing huge lip plugs, and they're pretty shy about meeting outsiders, so they continue to live in their ancient way. But in the 1980s, some Russian doctors managed to say hello, but we still don't know much about them.

Sentinelese - the Super Private Tribe: On a little island near India, there's a tribe called the Sentinelese. They're known for being the most secretive group out there. They use bows and arrows to hunt, and they don't like it when strangers come knocking. There are pictures of them shooting their bows and arrows at a curious helicopter! Who knows what they think of these peculiar flying objects? As they are so protective over their island we hardly know anything about their lives.

LONE AMAZON SURVIVOR

Picture this: a guy living all alone in the Amazon rainforest, like a real-life Tarzan! He's the last one of his tribe, so he became like a living book of all their secrets, like their language and how they live.

Vietnam War Discovery: During the Vietnam War, some folks called the Ruc people had to leave their caves because of bombs. They had to meet the modern world, and it caused a lot of trouble, especially with the Vietnamese government who wanted to move them to different places, while the tribe wanted to stay in their ancient homes.

Jackson Whites – the Stealthy Tribe: Back in the 1700s, while North America was being colonised, the Jackson Whites, a Native American tribe, managed to stay hidden through the whole century. They got their name because they had lighter skin than other tribes. Hide-and-seek champs!

92

DEATH RITUALS AROUND THE WORLD

People from all around the world have their special ways of honouring those who have passed away. Let's look at some of the most interesting customs. Learning and speaking about death, and seeing it as a natural stage in the circle of life, can allow us to live less fearfully.

Famadihana - Dancing with the Dead: In Madagascar, they open the tombs of their ancestors, wrap the bodies in new clothes, and have joyful dances to help them move on to the next life.

The Parade: In Varanasi, India, they celebrate someone's life by taking them on a parade through the streets. The body is dressed in colourful clothes, sprinkled with water from a sacred river, and then cremated on a fire. They believe the fire can help souls be freed from the cycle of life, death, and rebirth. It's like a big farewell party, guiding the person's soul to find peace.

Sky Burial: In Tibet they leave the body outside for birds and animals to eat. It's like sharing a meal with nature and helping the circle of life while also saying goodbye. It's thought to be a good sign if the whole body is consumed, as it's believed that vultures wouldn't touch the remains of someone who did evil deeds.

Tower of Silence: Zoroastrians of Iran and India have a unique idea. They believe that a body can make things impure, even the earth and fire. So, they place the body on a special tower for vultures to eat. But before that, they clean the body and remove any clothes.

93

Filipino Traditions: In the Philippines, different regions have their own special customs. Some dress up their loved ones, and others even put them in a chair. In Sagada, they hang coffins from cliffs to be closer to heaven. In Cavite, people are often buried upright within a chosen hollowed-out tree.

Scattering Ashes at Sea in Hong Kong: In Hong Kong, many people choose cremation when someone passes away because there isn't much space for traditional burials. But finding a place to keep the urn is tough. They don't usually bring urns home because it mixes the worlds of the living and the dead. So, the government encourages families to scatter ashes in special gardens or at sea. They even provide free ferry rides to these places.

Ghana's Fantasy Coffins: In Ghana, they believe that the dead still have power and can help their living family members. So, they make sure to please them. They think the person will continue their job even after death, so they make special coffins that show what the person did when they were alive. These coffins can be in all kinds of shapes, like shoes, boats, or even drink bottles.

Modern Mummies of Papua New Guinea: In Papua New Guinea, the Anga tribe still practises an ancient tradition – mummification. They do this to make sure the person's memory lives on and to protect their family. To mummify someone, they smoke their body for three months to stop it from rotting. They also make sure no part of the body, including fluids and organs, touches the ground. Once the person is mummified, they sit on a cliff and watch over the village, even after they're gone.

94

Ashes to Beautiful Beads: In South Korea, they take the ashes of the person who passed away and turn them into pretty beads. These beads can be put on display in vases or bowls, which is a lovely way to remember someone. It's like turning memories into art.

IKWA OZU

Nigeria's 'Second Burials': In Nigeria, when someone passes away, it's not seen as the end but a transition. After the first burial, they have a 'second burial' called 'ikwa ozu' to help the person join their ancestors. These ceremonies can be extremely fancy and last for days, with lots of drinks and entertainment. Sometimes, they even have pretend trials to figure out what caused the death. Some also choose to eat the person's favourite food all day to share it with them in the afterlife.

Water Burial: Some people, like those in the Nordic regions, have a deep connection with water. They may put coffins high up on cliffs or let them float away in 'death ships.' It's their way of giving back to nature and their gods.

In the Indonesian Tana Toraja tribe, babies who die before they start teething are buried in the hollow of a living tree. As the tree grows, it absorbs the child. Dozens of babies may be interred in a single tree. The tribes people believe that the tree will waft away their souls.

95

PROVERBS FROM AROUND THE WORLD

YUP

A proverb is an important life lesson in short, poetic phrase. You might recognise some of these as they're often repeated and passed down through the generations. Looking at other countries' proverbs is like being given a bundle of wisdom that crosses boundaries in time and space.

'Shared joy is a double joy; shared sorrow is half a sorrow.' — **Swedish Proverb**

When you celebrate joyful moments with someone, the happiness doubles as you both experience it together. Similarly, when you're going through a difficult time, sharing your sorrow with a friend or loved one can help lighten the burden.

'Do good and throw it in the sea.' — **Arab Proverb**

This saying suggests that acts of kindness and good deeds should be done without expecting anything in return. You do good because it's the right thing to do, not for personal gain or recognition.

'A pen can be mightier than a sword.' — **English Saying**

This saying highlights the influence of words and written ideas. It suggests that words have the power to change the world and shape our thoughts.

'A man who uses force is afraid of reasoning.' — **Kenyan Proverb**

This saying points out that violence or force is often a response born out of fear or an inability to resolve conflicts through peaceful and rational means.

● ● ● ● ● ● ● ● ● ● ● ● ● ●

'If you can walk, you can dance; if you can talk, you can sing.' — **Zimbabwe proverb**

This proverb encourages us not to fear imperfection. It suggests that we can enjoy activities even if we don't do them perfectly.

IF YOU WANT TO GO FAST, GO ALONE, IF YOU WANT TO GO FAR, GO TOGETHER

African Proverb

This proverb suggests that while you can achieve things quickly on your own, the real journey and accomplishments come when you work together with others. Going far requires the collective efforts and strengths of a group.

'It takes a whole village to raise a child.' — **African proverb**

Parents can use all the help they can get in raising children, and this saying reflects the idea that every person in a community contributes to a child's growth and well-being.

● ● ● ● ● ● ● ● ● ● ● ● ●

"Ignorance is nothing to be ashamed of; the real shame is in refusing to learn.' — **Russian proverb**

This proverb teaches us that it's okay not to know everything, as long as we remain open to gaining knowledge. Rejecting opportunities to learn is where the real problem lies.

"Fall seven times, stand up eight.' — **Japanese proverb**

This Japanese saying teaches us the importance of persistence. It reminds us that success often requires multiple attempts, and we should never give up.

'Turn your face toward the sun, and the shadows will fall behind you.' — **Maori proverb**

This saying promotes optimism and positive thinking. It suggests that as we focus on brighter things, darkness and negativity will fade away.

'Begin to weave, and God will provide the thread.' — **German proverb**

This proverb encourages us to have faith in our dreams and take the first steps towards our goals. It suggests that action, determination, and focus attract the resources we need.

The work praises the man' — **Irish saying**

This saying emphasises the importance of doing quality work. When you excel at what you do, your work itself becomes your best advocate.

"A man may learn wisdom even from a foe.' — ***Greek proverb***

Sometimes, we learn valuable lessons from difficult situations or people we disagree with. This proverb encourages us not to dismiss knowledge based on its source.

'It's not enough to learn how to ride, you must also learn how to fall.' — ***Mexican proverb***

This saying encourages us to accept both failure and success as part of the same journey. Being gracious in both victory and defeat is essential.

"Words should be weighed, not counted.' — **Yiddish Proverb**

This encourages us to choose our words carefully, considering their impact and meaning, rather than aiming to say the most or have the last word. It's a reminder to speak thoughtfully.

• • • • • • • • • • • • • •

"Where love reigns, the impossible may be attained.' — **Indian Proverb**

Love has the power to conquer obstacles and make seemingly impossible things achievable. When there's genuine love and support, people can overcome challenges and accomplish remarkable feats.

ITS BETTER TO LIGHT A CANDLE
THAN CURSE THE DARKNESS

Chinese Proverb
This proverb encourages proactive problem-solving. Instead of complaining or being negative about a difficult situation, it's more productive to take positive actions to make things better.

"He who does not travel, does not know the value of men.' — ***Moorish Proverb***

Travelling exposes you to different cultures, experiences, and people. This proverb implies that by staying in one place, you limit your understanding of the diversity and value of humanity.

• • • • • • • • • • • • •

"'Change yourself and fortune will change with you.' — ***Portuguese Proverb***

This saying emphasises personal responsibility and growth. It suggests that by working on self-improvement and making positive changes in your life, you can influence your fate and create a better future.

'Give a man a fish, and you feed him for a day. Teach a man to fish, and you feed him for a lifetime.' — **Chinese Proverb**

This proverb stresses the importance of education and self-sufficiency. Providing someone with skills and knowledge is more valuable than just helping them temporarily.

● ● ● ● ● ● ● ● ● ● ● ● ●

'If you take big paces, you leave big spaces.' — **Burmese Proverb**

Taking measured and careful steps can help avoid making mistakes. If you move too quickly, you might miss important details or create gaps in your progress.

● ● ● ● ● ● ● ● ● ● ● ● ●

'Don't sail out farther than you can row back.' — **Danish Proverb**

This proverb advises caution and preparation. Just like you wouldn't want to venture too far out to sea without knowing you can row back to safety, it's smart not to take risks that you can't easily undo.

● ● ● ● ● ● ● ● ● ● ● ● ●

'Measure a thousand times and cut once.' — **Turkish Proverb**

This proverb advises against rushing into things and advocates for thorough consideration. It's wise to carefully plan and think things through.

● ● ● ● ● ● ● ● ● ● ● ● ●

A FAULT CONFESSED IS HALF REDRESSED

- Zulu Proverb

Acknowledging your mistakes is the first step toward making amends and finding a solution. Confessing a fault is a significant part of correcting it.

'Deep doubts, deep wisdom; small doubts, small wisdom.' — **Chinese Proverb**

Questioning and doubting can lead to greater understanding and wisdom. When you delve deeply into your uncertainties, you're more likely to uncover profound insights.

● ● ● ● ● ● ● ● ● ● ● ● ●

'Character is always corrupted by prosperity.' — **Icelandic Proverb**

This proverb suggests that having too much wealth or success can sometimes negatively influence a person's character or integrity. It's a reminder to stay grounded even in prosperity.

A BEAUTIFUL THING IS NEVER PERFECT

— **Egyptian Proverb**

Beauty doesn't require perfection. In fact, imperfections can enhance beauty, making it unique and interesting.

'To be willing is only half the task.' — **Armenian Proverb**

Willingness is an important start, but it's essential to follow through with action. Having the intention to do something is only part of the journey.

● ● ● ● ● ● ● ● ● ● ● ● ●

'No man can paddle two canoes at the same time.' — **Bantu Proverb**

Trying to do two conflicting things simultaneously often results in inefficiency and a lack of progress. Concentrating on one task at a time usually leads to better outcomes.

101

'Beauty lies in the eye of the beholder.' — **English Proverb**

This saying reminds us that beauty is a subjective concept. What one person finds beautiful, another may not. It's all about individual perspective.

Two wrongs don't make a right.' — **English Proverb**

This saying advises against responding to a wrongdoing with another wrongdoing. It's a reminder that addressing a mistake with another mistake doesn't lead to a positive outcome.

'In a battle between elephants, the ants get squashed.' — **Thai Proverb**

This proverb highlights the idea that when powerful individuals or groups clash, it's often the smaller, less influential ones who suffer the most.

* * * * * * * * * * * * *

'Before you score, you first must have a goal.' — **Greek Proverb**

To achieve something, you need to set a clear goal or target. Scoring or succeeding comes after you've established what you want to accomplish.

* * * * * * * * * * * * *

What you see in yourself is what you see in the world.' — **Afghan Proverb**

Our perception of the world is often shaped by our self-perception. If you see positivity and goodness in yourself, you're more likely to see it in others and the world around you.

* * * * * * * * * * * * *

'A large chair does not make a king.' — **Sudanese Proverb**

The size or grandeur of one's possessions or position doesn't necessarily define their worth or character. Being truly noble isn't about outward appearances.

102

THE OLD
WORLD

This is where history unfolds its mysterious tales. We're going to discover the secrets of the past, explore what's changed over the last 1000 years, and embark on a quest for long-lost treasures.

NO CHANGE IN 1000 YEARS

You know the saying, 'Some things never change'? Well, it's never been more true than for this collection of factoids!

Ancient Graffiti: Believe it or not, people in ancient times left their mark through graffiti too! Sometimes, their messages sound surprisingly modern. It's a reminder that humans have always been, well, human.

Sandals: Sandals have been protecting our feet for ages. They've adapted to different cultures and styles, but the general idea remains the same. You could probably wear Roman-style sandals with a summer outfit today and it would still look ok!

Physical Humour: People have always enjoyed a good laugh, and some things never get old. We've been chuckling at funny faces, slips, and even unexpected toots for as long as we can remember.

Storytelling Tradition: Our love for stories is timeless. Humans have been sharing tales about the world since the birth of speech. It's heartwarming to know that this tradition has stuck around through the millennia, even though some stories have disappeared over the years.

Generational Judgments: One thing that hasn't changed over the ages? People judge other generations, whether older or younger. It seems like critiquing each other is a tradition of its own!

Sheep Shearing: Shearing sheep has pretty much stayed the same for thousands of years. Even with modern tools, the basic technique hasn't changed much.

Using Mortar and Pestle: You know that grinding and mixing thing with a mortar and pestle? It's been around forever, connecting us to our cooking history.

Parent-Child Bond: Parents have always cared for their little ones with such tenderness. Whether it's breastfeeding, gazing, cuddling, playing, or speaking softly to babies, these timeless rituals haven't changed much over the centuries.

Traditional Crafts: Skills like pottery, textiles, stained glass, and leatherworking have been around for a long time. The tools and techniques might have evolved a bit, but the crafts themselves remain pretty consistent.

Taxes Through Time: Taxes, believe it or not, have been around forever. Whether it's ancient consumption taxes or modern property and tariff taxes, they've always been part of how societies work economically.

Timeless Tools: Tools like knives, hammers, axes, and scissors have kept their basic designs and functions from way back when to now.

Furry Companions: Cats and dogs have been our furry pals for centuries. They've stuck around as pets, offering their companionship.

BIGGEST CHANGES IN 1000 YEARS

Here's a rundown of the last 10 centuries along with the changes that rocked humanity.

Eleventh Century: Building Castles
Picture this: a thousand years ago, Europe didn't have many castles. It was like open land ready for anyone to conquer. But in the eleventh century, lords decided to build these massive fortresses. It made it super tough for kings to take over their neighbours. So, instead of conquering, lords started focusing on ruling and protecting their territories. Big change, right?

Twelfth Century: Law and Order
Now, let's jump to the twelfth century. This is when things got legal! They introduced systematic laws, legal books, and trial procedures. 'Justices in eyre' (early circuit judges) and trial by jury came into play. It was like setting up rules for everyone to follow. This made societies work smoother and deal with problems in a fair way.

Thirteenth Century: Money Matters
Back then, people didn't use money much. It was all about swapping stuff. But in the thirteenth century, markets started popping up everywhere. Trade and business took off. Coins started circulating, and banks began offering credit. Money became a big deal, and it changed how societies worked.

Fourteenth Century: The Plague

Time for a dark chapter. The plague hit, and it was devastating. Almost half the people vanished in just months! Afterwards, survivors had better lives, and folks started thinking differently about faith, sickness, and being humble.

Fifteenth Century: Columbus's Discovery

Now, we're sailing with Columbus! He discovered lands that were new to the western world and shook up what people knew about the world. It made everyone curious and made them question old beliefs. Science started to gain trust.

Sixteenth Century: Less Fighting

Good news! In the sixteenth century, people started fighting less. They learned to read and write better, which helped them communicate and understand each other. Trust in science grew, so they went to doctors instead of believing in superstitions.

Seventeenth Century: Scientific Revolution

Science showed how it could replace superstition. Old beliefs, like the Earth being the centre of everything, got replaced by researched and proven ideas. It was like switching from suspicion to facts.

Eighteenth Century: French Revolution

In 1789, the French Revolution changed the game. People began to talk about equality, women's rights, and making society better. These ideas echoed through the nineteenth century, pushing for big social changes.

Nineteenth Century: Communication Revolution

Time for a tech leap! In the nineteenth century, telegraphs, railways, and telephones made messages travel crazy fast. Before, the fastest news could travel was by horse! This changed how governments worked and how info was shared.

Twentieth Century: Future Thinking

Finally, the twentieth century! Technology like the internet rocked the world, but people also started planning for the future. They thought more about weather predictions, housing, and resources, and also started to think about how to change things to leave the planet in a better way for the future.

THE INCAS

Long, long ago in a land called Peru, there were some people called the Incas. These guys were pretty smart and built amazing things that even the mighty Spanish conquistadors couldn't figure out!

They believed in a Sun god named Inti, who was a big deal in their tribe. They built temples to honour him, like the famous Temple of the Sun in Machu Picchu.

During the Winter Solstice the sun would shine through a window in the Temple of the Sun and create a perfect rectangle of light around the altar. And during the Summer Solstice the sun did the same thing through a different window.

They built massive walls at places like Sacsayhuaman using gigantic rocks that weighed more than 91 tonnes (100 imperial tons)! Can you imagine that?

They shape the rocks with bronze tools, and then move them with ropes, logs, and poles. They fitted the rocks together so perfectly that they didn't even need mortar. They even had special stones with lots of angles that acted like locks to hold everything in place. Talk about clever engineering!

These buildings were so well-made that even earthquakes couldn't knock them down. The stones could move a little during a tremor, but then they would settle right back into place once the shaking stopped. Over 500 years have passed and we're still in awe of their engineering skills!

AT THE SAME TIME?!

We normally keep history's timelines very separate. Why study the advances in space travel alongside the evolution of suitcase technology? But that's exactly why it can blow our minds when we compare dates for unrelated topics. Check out these examples of things you won't believe happened at the same time.

Homo Sapiens, Neanderthals, and Komodo Dragons: Our species, Homo sapiens, lived alongside Neanderthals. But it gets even more interesting – tiny people known as *Homo floresiensis* (the 'Hobbit') were around on an Indonesian island until about 50,000 years ago. They might have met our ancestors. And, guess what, enormous Komodo dragons were part of the same world! So, we have humans, 'Hobbits,' Neanderthals, and Komodo dragons all in one period in history.

Twentieth Century: Future Thinking 9/11 vs. Berlin Wall: The sad events of September 11, 2001 (9/11) are now longer ago than the period between then and the fall of the Berlin Wall in 1989. It reminds us that history moves fast and we should remember important moments.

Moon Landing and Wheelie Suitcases: Humans walked on the moon during the Apollo 11 mission in 1969, but it wasn't until the 1970s that people started using suitcases with wheels. The moon landing was a giant leap for space exploration, and wheelie suitcases were a small step for travellers who preferred to stay on Earth!

Woolly Mammoths and the Pyramids:
When the ancient Egyptians were building the pyramids, huge, furry creatures called woolly mammoths were still roaming around. The pyramids were constructed about 4,500 years ago, and woolly mammoths stuck around for thousands of years after the Ice Age. Imagine mammoths and pyramids at the same time. Not in the same place though, that would be crazy!

Pyramids and the Roman Empire: The famous pyramids in Egypt were already very old when the mighty Roman Empire was at its height. The pyramids were built over 2,000 years before the Romans ruled. It's a fascinating reminder of how long ago those pyramids were constructed!

1889 Events: In 1889, several noteworthy events occurred. The Eiffel Tower in Paris was completed, the Wall Street Journal started publishing, Vincent van Gogh painted 'Starry Night,' Coca-Cola was founded, Nintendo began as a playing card company and Adolf Hitler was born. Lots of things were happening in that year!

Huxley, Lewis, and Kennedy: On November 22, 1963, three important people from different fields passed away: Aldous Huxley, known as the author of 'Brave New World,' C. S. Lewis, the writer of 'The Chronicles of Narnia,' and John F. Kennedy, the 35th US President. It's like the universe had a plan for that day!

Coca-Cola and Italy: Coca-Cola, the famous drink, is only 31 years younger than Italy as we know it today. It shows that some brands and inventions are now older than entire countries.

Anne Frank and Martin Luther King Jr.: Anne Frank, a Jewish girl who wrote a famous diary during the Second World War, and Martin Luther King Jr., a leader in the fight for civil rights, were born in the same year, 1929. Anne's story reflects the horrors of the Holocaust, while Martin's work promoted equality and justice.

Roman Empire and Columbus: The Eastern Roman Empire ended just 40 years before Christopher Columbus voyaged to the Americas. Imagine being a surviving Roman and hearing about a whole new continent!

Spain's Dictatorship and Microsoft: Spain still had a dictator named Francisco Franco until the late 1970s, while Microsoft started in 1975.

CLEOPATRA, MOON LANDINGS AND PYRAMIDS

Cleopatra lived closer to the moon landings of 1969 than to the building of the ancient Pyramids of Giza, despite being an ancient Egyptian. Wow! That shows just how long the ancient Egyptians existed.

1912 Events: In 1912, the Titanic sank, a huge tragedy. But it's also the year vitamins were discovered, and scientific things like X-rays were invented. A mix of sad and smart!

1918 Flu and the First World War: The 1918 flu pandemic was more deadly than the First World War, which ended in the year the pandemic began. It was even deadlier than the Black Death.

Wild West and Victorian Britain:
While the American Wild West was wild and free, far away in Victorian Britain, there was a time of industry, change, and elegance. It's like two very different worlds at the same time!

Constantinople and Columbus: Constantinople fell to the Ottoman Empire in 1453. Then, in 1492, Christopher Columbus was the first Westerner to voyage to the Americas. People who lived through these times saw the end of an ancient empire and the start of a new world. It was a time of big change.

Marilyn Monroe and Queen Elizabeth II: Marilyn Monroe, a famous Hollywood actress, and Queen Elizabeth II, the current queen of the UK, were both born in the year 1926. They became well-known figures in their own right, each in very different ways.

Guillotine and Star Wars: The last time the guillotine was used in France was in 1977, which is the same year the very first Star Wars movie was released. The guillotine was used for executions, while Star Wars became a massive hit in the world of movies. Quite an unusual combination of events for one year.

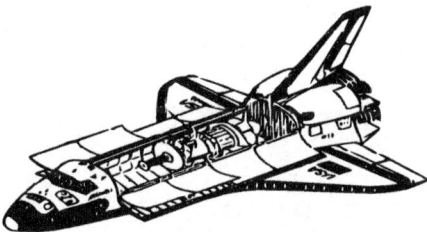

LONG LOST TREASURES

Throughout history, people have loved treasure. Some things of great value have gone missing over the years and you can bet that there are still people searching high and low for them. Are you ready to join a real-life treasure hunt?

George Mallory's Lost Camera

Imagine climbing a super tall mountain like Mount Everest, which is the tallest one in the world. A long time ago, a brave man named George Mallory tried to climb it. He had a camera with him to take pictures. But he and his friend never came back, and rescuers never found his camera either. The real mystery is that if someone ever finds the old camera, and there are photos of the top of Everest on there, then it would prove that George Mallory managed to get to the top of Everest nearly 30 years before the official world record!

The Enigmatic Copper Scroll Treasures

The Copper Scroll Treasure: Back in 1952, archaeologists found a copper scroll near the Dead Sea, along with the famous Dead Sea Scrolls. It talks about hidden treasures, but no one knows if the treasures are real or just make-believe. The writing on the scroll is super old, from around the year 700. Could the treasures possibly still exist after such a long time?

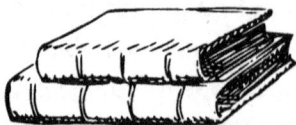

The Vanishing Library of Moscow Tsars

There's a story that the Moscow Tsars had this magical library with tons of important ancient books and maps, especially in Greek. Some people say the library might not even exist, but others are still looking for it. Even though they haven't found the whole library, they did discover some of those ancient books in other places.

The Lost Sarcophagus of Menkaure

Inside an Egyptian pyramid built for the ancient king Menkaure, a fancy coffin called a sarcophagus was discovered. It was beautifully engraved. But here's the mystery part: in 1838, someone tried to take this beautiful sarcophagus to England. They put it on a ship called Beatrice, but the ship sank, and the sarcophagus is still somewhere under the sea. To find it, someone has to discover the shipwreck, and divers have been trying until this day.

The Elusive Ark of the Covenant

A long, long time ago, there was a super sacred chest called the Ark of the Covenant. It held the Ten Commandments: a set of principles that play a big part in Judaism, Christianity, and Islam. It was housed in a specially-made temple in Jerusalem. But, the Babylonians came and destroyed that temple in 587 B.C. Since then, nobody knows where the Ark went. It's like a big puzzle waiting to be solved. Some think it might be in Babylon or buried in Jerusalem. There's even a story saying it might reveal itself when the right time comes, but we're waiting to find out.

The Missing Honjo Masamune Sword

Picture a super cool sword – a curved, beautiful Samurai sword to be exact. This sword belonged to a famous mediaeval Japanese swordmaker named Masamune and was named after a guy called Honjo Shigenaga. It was passed down through the years, but during the Second World War, it had to be given to the Americans. The problem is, nobody knows where it is now! It might have been lost or taken to the US, and it's a real mystery.

The Vanishing Florentine Diamond

A long time ago in Europe, there was a super special diamond from India that was yellow and huge – 137 carats! The average diamond engagement ring is around one carat. People think the Florentine Diamond was with a duke who took it into battle, but after the First World War, it went to an emperor. The story gets a little tricky here because no one knows exactly what happened to it after that. Some people say it might have been cut into smaller diamonds or maybe it's still out there somewhere…

The Stolen Crown Jewels of Ireland

In Ireland, some very fancy jewels belonged to a group of knights chosen by the UK royal family. There were sparkling stars, shiny brooches, and golden collars, but they were stolen in 1907 from Dublin Castle. Thieves took them because there wasn't good security, and no one knows where the jewels went. People have ideas about who might have taken them but there's never been any solid evidence. Innocent until proven guilty!

The Disappearing Da Vinci Mural

Leonardo da Vinci was a famous artist who painted a masterpiece on a wall in Italy. It was a big battle scene called the Battle of Anghiari. But then, another artist covered it up with his own painting. In 2012, some experts said they found da Vinci's painting hiding under the other one, but they couldn't be sure. Is it there or not?

First-Century Gospels

Some people think there were special books about Jesus and his teachings written in the first century. That's right after he lived! They found a tiny piece of one of these books on the face mask of an Egyptian mummy (of all places!), and it got everybody excited. But then, they realised it was too old to be one of the lost gospels. So, we're still waiting to find those special books.

Sappho's Lost Poems

Imagine a famous poet from ancient Greece, like a rock star of her time. This poet was named Sappho, and her poems were read throughout the land. But guess what? Most of her poems disappeared. They vanished into thin air! People only found a few of them. In 2014, they thought they found two more, but then in 2021, they said maybe they didn't find them after all. So, where are the rest of Sappho's poems? It's still a big question mark. Over 2500 years later, her surviving poems continue to be powerful and meaningful for the modern-day reader.

The Mysterious Dead Bishop's Treasure

A long time ago, a ship called São Vicente was filled with treasures from a bishop who passed away. There was gold, silver, jewels, tapestries, and more. Some pirates attacked the ship, and one group of pirates got caught, but the other group just disappeared with all the treasure. Nobody knows what happened to them or where the treasures ended up. Shiver my timbers!

The Stolen Art of Isabella Stewart Gardner Museum

In 1990, two thieves pretended to be police officers and stole a bunch of really famous and valuable art from a museum in Boston, worth around half a billion dollars! The funny thing is, they never caught the thieves, and nobody knows where the art went. It's like it vanished in a puff of smoke!

The Lost Romanov Easter Eggs

Picture a bunch of fancy Easter eggs made of gems and other precious materials. These eggs were specially crafted for kings and queens in the Russian Romanov family. In 1918, the family was killed by people against the monarchy and the eggs vanished. Some people say the eggs might be in other countries now, but nobody really knows. Maybe they're in private collections all around the world.

The Legendary Nazi Gold of Lake Toplitz

During the Second World War, some people said the Nazis hid a bunch of gold in a lake in Austria. They thought it was so important that they sunk it to keep it safe. But even though people have looked and looked in the lake, they *still* haven't found the gold. Some say it's because the lake is very deep and there are lots of other things that could be covering the treasure. The gold continues to be a big, shiny mystery!

Missing Caravaggio Painting

Caravaggio was a famous artist, and he painted a super impressive picture called 'Nativity with St. Francis and St. Lawrence.' But in 1969, it got stolen from a chapel in Italy. People say the disappearance could be connected to the mafia, but they haven't found it yet. In 2015, they put a copy of the painting back in the chapel to keep the memory alive.

The Enigma of the Q Source

Imagine a super old text about Jesus that's like a treasure map. This text is called the Q Source, and people think it had sayings from Jesus. The funny thing is, nobody has ever found this text. They just think it exists because parts of it are in other books about Jesus. Even though they haven't found it yet, they believe it's out there somewhere.

The Vanished Peking Man

In the Chinese city of Beijing, they found fossils of a special kind of human called Peking Man. It was like finding the secrets of our ancestors as it taught scientists about a stage of human evolution. But then, during the Second World War in 1941, those fossils disappeared. Some people think they were lost at sea on their way to the US. Others say they might be buried under a parking lot in China. Will Peking Man ever be rediscovered?

The Enigmatic Amber Room

Long ago in Russia, there was a room made of amber, a magical golden material that glowed and sparkled. This room, known as the Amber Room, was full of beautiful carvings, mirrors, and mosaics, and it was in the Catherine Palace near St. Petersburg. But during the Second World War, the German army came and took apart the entire Amber Room, piece by piece! The pieces were carried away to Germany, and the original Amber Room disappeared. Even today, no one knows where those pieces went.

The Missing Panel of 'The Just Judges'

Imagine a big painting in a fancy church in Belgium. It's part of a huge picture called the Ghent Altarpiece, and one piece of the painting is missing. This piece is called 'The Just Judges.' It was stolen in 1934, and no one has ever found it. Even though a lot of time has passed, people are still trying to find this missing piece. What a puzzle! Literally.

The Vanished Jules Rimet Trophy

The football World Cup trophy disappeared in Brazil after they won it three times. The thieves took it in 1983 and never gave it back. Some people think they melted it down to get the gold from it. But it's still missing, and nobody has seen it for a long time. What a disappointment for the players!

MYSTERIOUS ARCHEOLOGY

Holey Jar: Archeologists found a jar with lots of little holes in it from Roman times in London, England. It's a real head-scratcher because we're not sure what it was used for. Some folks think it might have been a lamp, a cage for fattening up edible dormice (yuck!), or to keep snakes in. But the real answer remains a bit of a guess.

Stone Spheres in Costa Rica: In the southern part of Costa Rica, there's a place called the Diquis Delta. It's home to these giant stone balls known as Las Bolas, made by people who lived there a very long time ago, maybe as far back as the year 600. The strange part is that no one is completely sure why they made these huge spheres. Some folks think they might have been used for looking at stars or giving directions, but we're still trying to figure it out.

Antikythera Mechanism: Imagine finding an ancient gadget that's more than 2,000 years old in the remains of a sunken Greek ship. This bronze device is full of tiny interlocking gears and weird writing. At first, people thought it was a super fancy compass, but it turns out it's an incredibly smart calendar for studying stars. The big question is who built it and why. It sounds like something out of a fantasy story!

Shroud of Turin: Imagine a piece of cloth that some folks believe was used to wrap Jesus Christ after he passed away. The story of this cloth goes way back to around the year 30. But there's a big mystery. When scientists used a special dating method, they found that the cloth might be from the thirteenth or fourteenth century. This has led to debates about its authenticity.

Göbekli Tepe: In 1994, a cool discovery happened in Turkey. They found a place called Göbekli Tepe, which is super ancient, around 10,000 years old! It's like the world's first known church. What's strange is that the folks who built it were hunters, not farmers. It's got archaeologists rethinking how our ancestors built stuff and why.

Cleopatra's Tomb: Cleopatra, the famous Egyptian queen, is known for her smarts and her relationships with important people like Julius Caesar and Mark Antony. But here's the puzzling part: no one knows where she and Mark Antony are buried. They were supposed to be laid to rest together near a temple of the goddess Isis, but the tomb location is a mystery. Long ago, thieves might have taken everything from their resting place.

Qin Shi Huang's Tomb: Imagine finding a whole army made of clay – that's what happened in China in 1974. This 'Terracotta Army' was meant to guard Emperor Qin Shi Huang even after he passed away.

The army holds more than 8,000 soldiers, 130 chariots with 520 horses, and 150 cavalry horses. But the Emperor's real burial place is still a big secret. There's a pyramid-shaped tomb near the clay army, but no one has explored it yet. This tomb is described in old stories as one of China's most amazing resting places for an emperor.

Atlantis: You might have heard stories about a special island called Atlantis that sank into the sea more than 10,000 years ago. People have lots of ideas about where it might be. Some say it's in the Bahamas, the Greek Islands, Cuba, or even Japan. But here's the deal: no one is certain if Atlantis was real or where it might be. What a great story to keep us wondering.

Stonehenge: In England, there's a famous spot called Stonehenge. It's super old, about 4,000 years! Nobody fully knows why it was built. Some say it was like an ancient telescope for watching stars, while others think it was a special place for healing. People have lots of ideas, but no one has the final answer. Thousands of tourists visit every year, especially for the summer solstice. Even today, it's considered a sacred site.

Super-Henge: Just near Stonehenge in the UK, there's something called Super-Henge. It's full of big stone pillars that were once standing upright. But we're not sure why it was built or what it was used for. It's like a mystery next to another mystery.

Ancient Animal Traps: In the deserts of places like Israel, Egypt, and Jordan, there are these strange old walls made of stones that aren't very noticeable from the ground but look like huge kites when you see them from above. Scientists were puzzled by these for a long time. Recently, they found out that these stone walls were used to help ancient people trap wild animals. Ingenious.

The Great Pyramids: You've probably heard of the pyramids in Egypt. They were built nearly 5,000 years ago, close to modern-day Cairo. But there's something we're still trying to figure out. Who built them and why? People keep exploring inside these huge pyramids and finding new tunnels and rooms looking for answers.

Noah's Ark: You've probably heard the story of Noah's Ark, a big boat that survived a huge flood. People have been searching for it near Mount Ararat in Turkey for a long time. But there's always been doubt about whether it exists. It's like a search that lives through the generations, just like the story itself.

The Lost Maya: The Maya civilization in Mexico and Central America was huge, but it suddenly fell apart around A.D. 900. There are many ideas about why this happened, like not having enough water or cutting down too many trees. But the real reason is still a huge mystery.

Voynich Manuscript: There's this super old book from the fifteenth century called the Voynich manuscript. It's full of strange writing and drawings of mythical plants and creatures, but no one can read it! Even top codebreakers haven't managed. It's like a secret code or a lost language. Some say it might even be a big joke from a long time ago. It's a fascinating puzzle that keeps researchers guessing.

The Khatt Shebib: In Jordan, there's a super long stone wall called the Khatt Shebib, and it's been puzzling scientists since 1948. It's not a wall for protection, but they think it might have marked a line between places where people grew crops and where animals roamed. It's like a hidden fence with a cool story.

The Big Circles: In Jordan, there are these giant stone circles dating back 2,000 years. They're huge and don't have openings for people or animals. But what they were used for is a big unknown. Why would these ancient folks have made these enormous circles?

King Tut's Death: You might have heard of King Tut, the young Egyptian pharaoh. But how he died is a mystery. It seems like he passed away suddenly. Some think it was from an infection or maybe a chariot accident. His tomb was also a bit rushed, which makes us wonder if it was meant for someone else. The plot thickens!

Nazca Lines: Over 2,000 years ago, in Peru, the Nazca people created these huge drawings on the ground that you can only see properly from way up in the sky. They were etched deeply into the desert sands.

Some of these drawings look like animals, plants, and strange figures. People couldn't agree on why they made them. Some thought it was to talk to aliens or study the stars. But now, most experts believe it was a way for the Nazca people to connect with their gods.

The Hobbits: Imagine finding tiny human-like bones on an island in Indonesia. That's what happened in 2003, and they named the little people Homo floresiensis. At first, folks thought they were humans with a condition, but it turns out they might be a whole different species. The question is where they fit in our family tree.

Underwater Cairn: In 2003, a huge structure made of stacked stones weighing about 60,000 tons was found underwater in the Sea of Galilee in Israel. But what it was for, we're still not sure. Some think it might have been for burials or it could be a structure that the sea covered over time. The mystery of its purpose continues.

The Cochno Stone: Imagine finding a giant stone in Scotland, known as the Cochno Stone, with swirling marks and strange holes. It's been a puzzle for ages. Some say it's art, while others think it could be linked to stars and the sky. The stars have always been important to humanity.

MYTHS AND

MYSTERIES

Prepare to be spellbound. In this chapter, we unravel a web of urban myths, venture into jungle mysteries, and explore the unexplained phenomena that continue to baffle our greatest minds.

URBAN MYTHS

Invented characters can capture our imagination so strongly, and their stories can get passed on so enthusiastically, that the line between fact and fiction gets blurry. Perhaps people want to believe these tales are true or to spook their friends and add some spice to life. Anyhow, you'll be glad to know this list is a load of old codswallop!

In Japan, there's a spooky legend about a young girl's spirit haunting school bathrooms. To make her appear, you have to go to the third-floor girls' bathroom, knock three times on the third stall, and ask if Hanako-san is there. How many students have been brave enough to try that one?

Heading to the Pine Barrens in South Jersey, US? Watch out for the Jersey Devil! It's often described as a hooved kangaroo-like creature with a goat-like head, a forked tail, and bat-like wings. It moves fast and makes a noise like a blood-curdling scream!

In Cornwall, England, there's a tale about a mysterious panther-like big cat. After 1978, folks started seeing it, and there were even stories of it attacking farm animals. They called it the Beast of Bodmin Moor!

Now, here's a wild one. Since the 1970s, there's been a story about a guy in Greenock, Scotland. They call him 'Catman' because they say he eats rats with his hands and takes care of wild cats. Gross!

Did you know there's a legend about a mythical village of dwarves in Waukesha County, Wisconsin, US? They call it Haunchyville and it's said to be fiercely protected against trespassers.

Travel back to the twelfth century to a village called Woolpit, England. Two kids with strangely coloured skin mysteriously showed up, and they were known as the Green Children. Never fear, they haven't been spotted since the 12th century.

Now, let's talk about Kushtaka – it's a Native American legend from Tlingit culture. These creatures can shapeshift and are like a mix of otters and people. They can make noises that sound like kids and wives in distress to lead fishermen astray, but they also help travellers who are lost in the wild or in danger at sea.

Watch out if you ever visit Escalante Petrified Forest State Park in Utah, US! There's a spooky story that says taking petrified wood from there will bring bad luck, make you lose your job, get sick, or even have accidents. That sounds like a terrible place for a picnic!

THE HAUNTED PAINTING

Have you heard of the painting called 'The Hands Resist Him' by Bill Stoneham from 1972? It's got a young boy and a doll in front of a glass door with lots of hands pressed against it. Some folks believe the characters in the painting move at night and even step out of the painting!

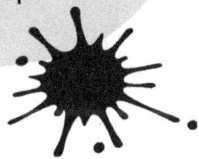

Here's a spooky one from Nigeria: Madam Koi Koi, a ghost that haunts boarding school dorms, hallways, and toilets at night. In regular schools, she hangs out in the bathrooms, especially if students come in too early or stay too late. She's often shown wearing a pair of red heels.

Ever heard about 'melon heads'? These are small creatures with big heads that sometimes pop up in remote parts of the US, like the Midwest, Northeast, and New England. People have lots of stories about them coming out of the woods to scare folks. Boo!

SPEEDY AGEING?

CHEESE LOVING?

EVERYDAY MYTHS: BUSTED!

People don't eat seven spiders a night, thank goodness! Spiders tend to stay away because they prefer dark, quiet spots and may be put off by our noisy snoozes.

Those old Greek and Roman statues? They used to be colourful! But over time, the paint wore off, so now they look all white. Some statues still have a bit of colour left so art historians can imagine what the figures used to be like.

Tutankhamun's tomb doesn't have a curse for anyone who messes with it. That whole curse thing was made up by newspapers in the 20th century!

You don't have to wait a whole day or 48 hours to report a missing person, despite what TV shows might say! If something's not right or someone's missing, it's super important to let the police know ASAP. The first 72 hours are crucial.

Santa Claus, the jolly man in red, wasn't made up by a soda company like Coca-Cola. People were already talking about Santa in his red outfit back in the late 1800s.

Fortune cookies might seem Chinese, but they're not. They were actually created in Japan and later brought to the US by the Japanese. In China, they're pretty rare.

Back in the Middle Ages, spices weren't used to hide the taste of spoiled meat. Spices were like fancy treats and only folks with good food could afford them. There's no proof they covered up bad meat.

Can you picture Buddha? You know, the chubby guy? His name's not really Buddha; it's Budai. He's a cool tenth-century Chinese folk hero also known as the Laughing Buddha, not the historical founder of Buddhism.

The Pyramids of Egypt weren't built by slaves. Skilled workers and regular folks, like farmers, helped build them. They got good food and didn't pay taxes, so it wasn't as bad as the stories say.

Romans didn't puke after meals on purpose. Those 'vomitoriums' in ancient Rome were just passageways to get in and out of stadiums, not places for food regrets!

Mediaeval folks weren't flat-earthers. They knew the Earth was round way back in 500 B.C. They were smarter than some myths give them credit for!

Julius Caesar wasn't born via C-section or 'caesarean section'. Back then, that would've been bad news for his mum. The word 'caesarean' probably comes from the Latin word for 'to cut.'

People in the Middle Ages didn't all die young. Sure, babies had it tough, but if you made it to your 20s, you could live a long time. A 21-year-old could hope for 64 years of life!

The Isaac Newton story of discovering gravity might not be real. He didn't say the apple hit his head. He just had a lightbulb moment while watching an apple fall.

John F. Kennedy wasn't talking about pastries in Berlin. His 'Ich bin ein Berliner' meant 'I am a Berlin citizen.' Pastries are just a yummy mix-up!

You can't see the Great Wall of China from space with the naked eye. City lights on Earth are way easier to spot from up there.

Vikings didn't name Iceland to scare people off. They just saw lots of ice and snow when they first arrived there. Greenland, though, got its name to trick folks into coming to live there. Over 80% of Greenland is covered in ice, but its grass was probably greener back in the summer of A.D. 982 when Erik the Red first landed in the southwest of the island. Sheep and potato farms still flourish in that same southwestern corner of Greenland, which sits further south.

Bulls don't care about the colour red. They're not big fans of it or anything. What makes them charge is feeling threatened, not the colour of a matador's cape.

Piranhas aren't all about meat. They swim together to stay safe, not to be mean. They rarely nibble on humans, mostly fingers and toes if they're feeling threatened.

Lemmings don't jump off cliffs on purpose. That idea comes from a fake Disney movie. Nobody's sure why folks believed it, but it's not true.

Giving a gentle touch to help save a stranded baby bird or egg won't make their mum abandon it. This is true for most animals, except maybe some rabbits.

Rice won't puff up birdies' tummies or make them explode, but it's not their favourite snack either. Best stick to bird food if you want to help them survive the winter.

Hippos don't make pink milk, their milk is plain old white or beige. However they do release a special liquid from their skin which helps protect them from the sun and keep them moisturised, and this liquid goes bright red in the sun.

Not all worms turn into two worms when cut in half. Only certain ones can do this trick. And even then, the tail end may grow another tail at the cut end, rather than a new head! Not very useful!

Old elephants don't sneak away to special graveyards to die. They usually stick with their herd or friends until the end.

Wolves don't howl at the moon. They howl to talk to their wolf buddies, to hunt or express their territory.

Houseflies hang around for a month or so. The whole only surviving 24 hours thing? That's more like mayflies!

132

Ostriches don't bury their heads in the sand when they're scared. However, if they feel they're in danger and can't escape they may flop to the ground and keep still, to try to blend into the background.

Napoleon wasn't super short. He was about average height for a French guy in 1800. His 'Little Corporal' nickname was just what his friends affectionately called him.

Peeing on jellyfish stings won't help. That's just a silly tale.

Sunflowers don't follow the sun like a sunflower GPS. They face one direction all day.

Earwigs aren't ear climbers, and their name isn't about ears at all!

Mice don't go nuts for cheese. They prefer sweet treats. The cheese thing? It's probably because people used to store cheese in a way that was accessible to mice.

Dogs don't grow old seven times faster than us. It depends on their breed. Most dogs are like teenagers by their first birthday. Smaller ones grow up slower.

We didn't come from chimps. Humans and chimps both came from an ancient ape ancestor, about 6–8 million years ago, but then evolved down different paths. Chimpanzees and gorillas are still some of our closest relatives in the animal kingdom though!

Yep, we are animals too! Even though we usually only use the word 'animal' for our furry friends. However, the special human skills of communicating complex ideas, controlling our environment and working together in large groups are some things that set us apart.

Surprise! Urine isn't sterile in the bladder.

Cockroaches might handle radiation better than some, but they're not invincible.

Don't worry about the supervolcano in Yellowstone. It's not overdue to erupt.

The Earth's inside isn't all molten rock. There are solid parts in the centre too!

Fossil fuels don't come from dino bones. They're made from ancient sea critters and plants.

Our blood is red, not blue. Veins just look different under our skin.

The Bermuda Triangle isn't an extra mysterious place that causes ships to sink more often. It's just a regular part of the ocean with a normal number of shipwrecks.

You don't have to drink exactly eight glasses of water a day. Our needs change with our size, what we're doing and where we are.

Rust doesn't cause tetanus. The germs that do are found in dirty spots.

Bananas aren't radioactive, even though they have potassium-40. They're yummy and safe to eat!

Men and women have the same number of ribs even though that's not what the story of Adam and Eve says.

Water in sinks and toilets doesn't spin because of Earth's spin. It's more about how it enters and the shape of the bowl.

We use way more than just 10% of our brains. That is a pure myth!

Quicksand isn't like in adventure movies. People don't sink all the way in, but it's still tricky to get out.

Glass is a solid, not a liquid. It gets gooey only at super-high temps.

Most diamonds aren't squished coal, they are made when the element carbon is heated and squashed for millions of years deep in the earth. Coal is mostly made of ancient plants and contains a lot of carbon too, but diamonds were created way before plants even existed on Earth. Asteroids hitting the earth can also create diamonds.

Covering your head will keep you warmer, but it's no more important than covering any other part of your body. This myth is just a mix-up from an old study.

Climate change is mostly because of people burning stuff, destroying ecosystems and chopping down trees. Almost all scientists agree!

HELPFUL GHOSTS

There's no way to verify these sightings, but the stories are fun. Let's go and meet some not-so-scary ghosts!

Mollie Woodruff lived her whole life in a house in Tennessee, US that's now a museum. People who visit the museum say that Mollie's spirit is still there, being super helpful. She gives directions to the museum staff on how to arrange the furniture, checks up on guests, and even cleans up.

Let's hear about the Gray Man. Don't let the name scare you because he's a super helpful ghost. Whenever a big storm is about to hit South Carolina, US, this ghostly young man appears. He warns people to leave and find shelter, and he even protects houses from getting wrecked. It's like having a ghostly policeman watching over everyone.

Once upon a spooky night, a young nurse named Ruby was working at a hospital in the US. She was feeling overwhelmed with her new job when an older nurse named Martha appeared and told her to check on a patient in room eight. Turns out, the patient needed help, and Ruby saved the day! The same thing happened a few more times, where Martha would alert Ruby to situations where patients seriously needed help. But here's the twist: Martha had died thirty years ago! Yet, there are many stories of her appearing to help out new nurses and check on patients during night shifts!

Point Ormond in Australia has a cool history and a friendly ghost!
A young boy's spirit hangs out there and one time, he saved another kid from falling off a cliff. He woke up the napping mum and told her to call her son away from danger, just before the cliff collapsed.

136

Let's take a trip to Russia and meet a little hairy guy called a Domovoi. He's like a house spirit that comes with the home to keep things tidy and peaceful. He's super awesome because he can even transform into a pet or a former owner of the house. Just make sure to treat him well with bread, porridge, or salt. No bad manners or bad language, okay? If you don't follow the rules, the unhappy Domovoi might start causing a ruckus, like a mischievous poltergeist.

Here's a cool story about a ghost that made a family rich. In England, there was a family called the Nutts. In 1764 the oldest daughter, Ann, started seeing a ghost in their house. This ghost kept saying that something valuable was hidden there. So, the family searched and searched, but they couldn't find anything at first. But Ann and her ghost friend didn't give up!

Finally, the ghost pointed to a special stone in the house. When they lifted it, they found a secret pot hidden underneath. And you know what was inside? Almost two hundred shiny silver coins! The family became rich, all thanks to the helpful ghost.

Get ready to go underground with the tommyknockers! These little dudes are legends among miners in England and Wales. They live in mines and can make life easier or harder for the miners. They have a greenish colour and wear miner outfits. They enjoy jokes and sometimes steal tools and food, but they're also friendly enough to warn miners of danger. They even knock on walls to tell them about potential cave-ins. Miners are so grateful that they share the last bite of their pasties with the tommyknockers. It's their way of saying thanks!

Avery in The Pink Palace in Louisville, US, is a proper gentleman ghost who protects the people who live in the mansion. When the building turned into apartments, strange things started happening. Avery would appear right before accidents were about to happen, like fires. He would warn the residents and keep them safe from harm.

ISLAND MYSTERIES

Over in Corsica, a beautiful French island, there's a strange animal called a 'cat-fox.' It's not your usual kitty, though! These cat-foxes are bigger, with rings on their tails and dog-like teeth. They even have short whiskers and big ears!

For a long time, people didn't know much about these cool cat-foxes. But in 2012, some wildlife rangers decided to do some tests to learn more. Scientists checked the fur and found out that these cat-foxes were not just regular wild cats. They were a whole new species that nobody knew about. Their DNA was unique and didn't match any other animal on Earth. But it was a bit similar to a cat from Africa's forests.

Some people think that these cat-foxes might have been brought over by farmers thousands of years ago. What a long time to stay undiscovered.

There's an island in Japan called Okunoshima, which was a testing site for toxic gases during the Second World War. They used rabbits in their tests, and sadly those gases went on to harm lots of people.

However, things changed! Nowadays, the island is like a bunny paradise. Cute rabbits hopping everywhere, and people love them and Okunoshima has become a major tourist attraction. No predators like dogs or cats are allowed there, so the rabbits live in safety.

Here's the mysterious part: nobody knows exactly where these bunnies came from! Some say school children rescued and released eight bunnies on the island a long time ago, and those rabbits had babies, and their families got bigger and bigger. Now, there are hundreds of bunnies hopping around, asking people for snacks!

On a Pacific island called Yap, they have these curious stones called rai stones. They're big limestone disks with a hole in the middle, and some are even bigger than a person! What were they used for? Money!

These stones were like special gifts for weddings, used for politics, and ransoms, and passed down as family treasures. But there was a tiny problem! Since they were so huge and heavy, it was tough to move them around. So, the islanders came up with a clever idea! They used an oral system, like storytelling, to keep track of who owned which stone and all the details of the trades.

You know what's super interesting? Even though these stones are hundreds of years old, their oral tradition is kinda like today's blockchain for cryptocurrencies! The blockchain is like an open accountant's records that show who owns what in the cryptocurrency world. Just like the Yapese islanders used their storytelling to keep things transparent and safe!

In the South Pacific, there's an island called Henderson, and guess what? It's completely empty. No people or factories! But something weird happened in 2017 when some researchers went there. They were super shocked to find so much plastic trash all over the island!

It was like a plastic explosion! They counted up to 671 pieces of plastic for every square metre. Can you imagine that? It was the highest number ever seen anywhere in the world! The island was weighed down with over 15 tonnes (17 imperial tons) of plastic! And guess what's even crazier? Every day, over 3,500 new plastic pieces washed ashore on just one of its beaches! But how did all that plastic end up on a remote island with no people? Well, the island is in this swirling current called the South Pacific Gyre. It's like a plastic highway where all the trash from different countries rides the current until it meets the island. Can you believe they found plastic from 24 different countries?

JUNGLE MYSTERIES

In the rainforest, spiders are spinning awesome silk structures called 'silkhenges'! These webs are like a silk version of Stonehenge in England. Researchers aren't sure which spider makes them, but they think it's to protect their eggs. These incredible designs have fascinated scientists, but they don't know everything about them yet. The silkhenges are found in different parts of the Amazon, and researchers are eager to unravel this delicate mystery!

In Peru, there's a tiny town with a burning secret – the Boiling River of Mayantuyacu! The water is so hot it can burn anything that touches it. People who fell in got third-degree burns in seconds! That's the most serious category of burn. But there's a twist! A local shaman says the river is sacred and has special healing powers. Scientists are fascinated by the scalding water. They don't know for sure why it's so hot, but some think it might be from deep underground heat. Maybe time will uncover the truth behind the Boiling River.

Long, long ago, humans went to South America and lived in the Amazon jungle. But we don't know much about them. In 2017, brave archaeologists found drawings in a cave deep in Colombia's jungle. These drawings showed animals like mastodons (huge elephant-like animals) and giant sloths! The drawings help scientists learn about the animals and how early people lived there. How amazing that those paintings lasted long enough to teach us something today.

ADVENTURE OF THE CENTURY

In 2012 in Mozambique, Africa, a brilliant butterfly expert named Dr Julian Bayliss found a hidden rainforest on top of a mountain. Incredible, huh? Dr Julian and his team explored the forest and discovered new plants and animals, even butterflies that he named after the mountain. They also found old clay pots from ancient times. A true modern-day adventure! Humans haven't explored all corners of the Earth just yet.

DEEP IN THE JUNGLE...

There's a mysterious creature called the Mapinguari. Amazon tribes have been talking about this giant sloth for centuries. Some say it's super tall, with matted hair and a stinky smell. Locals claim they've seen it with one eye or a snarled mouth on its stomach! Scientists have searched for evidence, but haven't found any traces yet. Some think it might be based on ancient sloths that lived long ago. The mystery of the Mapinguari keeps everyone wondering!

UNEXPLAINED BY SCIENCE

Mysterious Mars Secrets: Imagine seeing human-like footprints on Mars! That's what happened, and it got scientists scratching their heads. There are also these dark lines that show up when it gets warm on Mars. Nobody knows what's making them. Maybe secrets are hiding under the Martian surface. Could there have been life there in the ancient past?

Cows and Their Magnetic Sense: Did you know that cows graze (eat grass) while facing either north or south? It's like they have a built-in compass! Scientists are trying to figure out how animals like cows know which way is which.

Ancient Architectural Wonders: There are some really old buildings and artwork that make people wonder, like the Ajanta caves and the pyramids. They're so amazing that we're not sure how the people who made them were able to build them. It would be hard for us to build something similar even with modern technology!

Egyptian Mummies and Mystery Medicines: Egyptian mummies are like ancient puzzles. When scientists checked them, they found some weird substances in their bodies. One of them is a kind of drug that nobody can figure out, even with modern science. It's like finding an ancient medicine bottle with no label!

Search for Aliens: Everybody loves the idea of aliens from other planets. Some people even say they've seen spaceships and strange things in the sky. There are some hotspots for such stories, like Roswell in the US. But, even with all these stories, we still don't have solid proof that aliens exist.

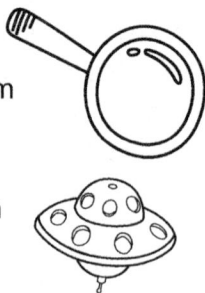

Bigfoot – The Elusive Ape-Man: Bigfoot is like a giant, hairy, ape-man with huge feet who's super hard to find. Lots of people say they've seen him in the North-West of the US, but there's no solid proof yet. There are pictures and videos but some people think they are fake.

Psychic Powers and Predictions: Some people seem to have superpowers, like predicting the future. Nostradamus was one of them. Some people think he made predictions that came true, like the Great Fire of London in 1666, and World Wars One and Two. Others think it was pure luck. In any case, scientists are doing their best to research these potential powers.

Near-Death Experiences: When people almost die, they sometimes say they saw and felt things even though they were unconscious. Sometimes they are technically dead if their heart stops, before doctors restart it. It's a big mystery because we don't really know what's happening, or how people could experience impossible things like floating out of their bodies.

The Universe's Big Bang: Scientists think the universe started with a huge explosion called the Big Bang. But what caused the Big Bang in the first place? That's a mystery we're still trying to solve.

THE VERY UNLIKELY

This is where the unbelievable becomes reality. We're taking a trip into the world of crazy coincidences, sporting triumphs that defy logic and stories of survival against the odds that will leave you in awe of life's most unexpected twists.

CRAZY COINCIDENCES

Imagine a meteor flying through space for billions of years, not hitting anything. Then, out of all the families in the world, it decides to crash into the house of the Commette family in France! Sounds like 'comet', get it?! It's the stuff of stories! Thankfully, no one was hurt, and now the Commettes have their very own piece of space rock. What a souvenir!

Once upon a time, there was a writer named Mark Twain, who wrote awesome books like The Adventures of Huckleberry Finn. He was a funny guy and liked to make people laugh. But here's something really cool about him: he was born in 1835, just two weeks after Halley's Comet paid a visit to Earth!

Now, what's Halley's Comet, you ask? Well, it's a special comet that zooms by our planet every 74-79 years. Mark Twain thought it was so special that he made a prediction. He said, 'When Halley's Comet comes back, I'll be ready to go too.' He thought it would be a big disappointment if he didn't leave this world when the comet returned.

Guess what? In 1910, Halley's Comet made another grand appearance. But on 21 April, the very next day, Mark Twain had a heart attack and passed away. It was like he knew it was his time to say goodbye, just as the comet was saying hello again.

FICTION PREDICTION

Let's dive into the world of books now. In 1898, a fantastic writer named Morgan Robertson wrote a novella called Futility. The story was about a ship called the Titan, and here's where it gets eerie. Just like the real Titanic, the Titan was described as unsinkable. And that's not all. Both ships had a big problem – they didn't have enough lifeboats. And guess what? They both collided with icebergs in the North Atlantic. It's almost like the writer had a crystal ball to see into the future!

There were twins from Ohio, US, who had no idea they were related.
They were separated at birth and went on to live their own separate lives.
Both of these twins were adopted by families who named them James.
Can you imagine? They grew up in different places, but both became
police officers when they grew up. What are the odds? And what
happened next? They both ended up marrying women named Linda!

But wait, there's more! Each twin had a son, and they named them James
Allan and James Alan. That's right, almost the same name! And to top it
off, they both had dogs named Toy. It's like they were living parallel lives
without even knowing it!

But the surprises don't stop there. Both brothers got divorced from their
first marriages. Can you guess what happened next? They both found
love again and ended up marrying women named Betty! It's just too much
to handle…

Once upon a time in New York, Stephen Lee and his fiancee Helen were
celebrating their engagement. They were looking at old family photos
when they made an amazing discovery. They found out that Helen's mum
and Stephen's dad had almost married each other in Korea many years
ago, but their parents didn't approve and they lost touch. By some crazy
chance, these two lovebirds from different parts of the world now have
grandchildren together. Love truly knows no boundaries!

Here's the tale of a brave cyclist named Maarten de Jonge. He must
have had some incredible luck or guardian angels watching over him.
First, he was supposed to be on a missing plane called Malaysia Airlines
Flight 370. He changed his plans and took an earlier flight instead. Phew,
close call! But Maarten was also supposed to be on another Malaysia
Airlines flight, Flight 17, which tragically got shot down over Ukraine. He
changed his plans once again, this time to save some money, and avoided
another disaster. Talk about a lucky escape!

Now, let's go back in time to the US Civil War era. John Wilkes Booth, the man who sadly shot Abraham Lincoln, had a brother named Edwin who was a famous stage actor and supported Abraham Lincoln's campaign to abolish slavery and create a strong central government.

One day, in a train station, something incredible happened. Lincoln's son, Robert Todd Lincoln, almost fell onto the train tracks, but Edwin Booth saved him just in time. The brother of the killer saved the son of the victim. That's nuts! Years later, they found out about this amazing connection.

WEIRD WARNING

It's time to talk about archaeology and a tomb they found. In 1940, Soviet archaeologists discovered the tomb of Tamerlane, a mighty conqueror. On the tomb, there was a warning that said opening it would bring an even worse invader. But the archaeologists were brave and ignored the warning. Guess what happened? Just three days later, Adolf Hitler launched Operation Barbarossa, the largest military invasion ever, against the Soviet Union. It's like the warning came true!

Once upon a time, there were three young men named Robby, David, and Eddie. They lived separate lives without knowing that they were identical triplets! They were adopted by different families, so they had no idea about each other.

But one day in 1980, two of the brothers ended up going to the same university by pure coincidence. The media heard about this incredible meeting and shared their story. And guess what happened next?

The third brother saw the news and reached out to them. It turns out that they were part of a special study by a psychologist who wanted to study whether personality traits are something people are born with, or whether they are created through the way children are raised. It's hard to believe they found each other after all those years!

Stephen Hawking was a super smart physicist and author. He was born on the exact same day that another famous scientist named Galileo died. And that's not all! When Stephen Hawking passed away, it was the birthday of yet another genius scientist named Einstein. Incredible timing!

But wait, there's more to Stephen Hawking's story. He had a disease called Lou Gehrig's Disease, which makes life tough. Most people who have it only live for about five years after they're diagnosed. Stephen Hawking beat the odds and lived for over 50 years with the disease! Wow! He used that time to teach us amazing things about the universe and make us laugh with his awesome sense of humour.

Thomas Jefferson and John Adams were two important figures in US history. They started off as friends, but then became rivals because of their political views. But in the end, they made up and stayed in touch through letters.

Now, here comes the incredible part. Thomas Jefferson and John Adams, the last two surviving members of the US revolutionaries who fought for independence, both died on the same day. And when did it happen? On 4 July! Yep, the same day North Americans celebrate that independence.

Now for a sweet and mysterious love story. Esther and Paul Grachan had just started dating when something strange happened. Paul was buying a sandwich and noticed that the dollar bill he was about to give the cashier had the name 'Esther' written on it. Can you imagine the surprise? It was like the universe was sending them a sign.

Paul decided to frame the dollar bill and give it to Esther as a special gift. She was so amazed and speechless when she saw it! Little did Paul know, Esther had written her name on that dollar and a few others after a breakup. She had a secret wish that the man who returned the dollar to her would be her future husband. It's like their love story was already written in the stars!

This is the story of a super lucky lady named Violet Jessop. She worked as a nurse and stewardess on ocean liners. You won't believe what happened to her! She survived not one, but two major ship accidents. First, she miraculously survived the sinking of the Titanic in 1912. And if that wasn't enough, she also survived the sinking of the Titanic's sister ship, the HMHS Britannic, in 1916. Talk about being 'Miss Unsinkable'! Oh, and she was even on board another ship, the RMS Olympic, when it had a collision but thankfully didn't sink.

A girl named Laura Buxton from England had an amazing adventure with a red balloon. She wrote her name and address on the balloon and let it go into the wind. Guess what? The balloon travelled 140 miles and landed near the yard of another girl named Laura Buxton!

They were both 10 years old and had so much in common. They looked alike, dressed alike, and even had the same pets. It was like they were long-lost twins! They decided to meet and had an incredible time discovering all their uncanny similarities. Who knew a balloon could bring two people together like that?

Once upon a beach, the Dubendorfs were having a nice walk with their dog. They were cleaning up the beach, picking up trash, when they found something special. It was a little bottle with a message inside! The message had the marriage vows of another couple, Melody Kloska and Matt Behrs, who had just got married on a beach across the lake. But that's not all! The Dubendorfs realised that the wedding date on the message was the same as their own beach wedding date. It was like a sign that their marriages were meant to be! They wrote a letter to congratulate the newlyweds. It was pretty surreal for everyone involved.

Here's another incredible story. The famous actor Anthony Hopkins needed to read a specific book for a movie role, but he couldn't find it anywhere. When he was sitting in a London Tube station, he spotted the exact book he was looking for! And not only that, it was even full of notes made by the author himself, George Feifer. What a weird day…

Michael and Lisa had been apart for over 10 years, and Michael really wanted to find his estranged daughter. So he came up with a clever plan. He reached out to a newspaper and asked them to publish a picture of him with his other two daughters, hoping that Lisa would see it and get in touch. And you know what? It worked!

When Lisa saw the picture, she realised something amazing. She and her mother were actually standing in the background of that very photo! Her dad had no idea that she was just yards away when the picture was taken. It was like a secret reunion captured in a single snapshot.

Here's something out of this world – solar eclipses! Have you ever seen the moon covering the sun? It's called a total solar eclipse, and it's an amazing sight. Even though the sun is much bigger than the moon, during an eclipse, they appear to be the same size. How does that happen? Well, it's all about the distance. The sun is about 400 times wider than the moon, but it's also 400 times farther away. That perfect balance makes the moon look just right to cover the sun during an eclipse.

Xu Weifang, who was 80 years old and had recent injuries, did something truly amazing. He saved an eight-year-old boy from drowning. That alone is incredible, right? But here's the twist: Xu found out that 30 years earlier, he had saved the boy's father from drowning too!

Let me tell you about Major Walter Summerford, a brave British soldier. One day, while fighting in Flanders in 1918, lightning struck him and paralyzed his legs. Ouch! In 1924, while he was peacefully fishing, lightning struck a tree right where he was sitting. The tree fell on him and paralyzed the right side of his body. How unlucky!

Now, here comes the weirdest part. In 1930, six years after his last lightning accident, Major Walter Summerford was taking a stroll in a park when lightning struck him once again! This time, it left him permanently paralyzed. Sadly, he passed away two years later. But guess what? Even after he was buried and resting in peace, lightning struck his tombstone! Talk about an electrifying coincidence!

149

And get ready for an unbelievable story about a French poet named Émile Deschamps. When he was a teenager, he met a guy named Mr. de Fortgibu who introduced him to plum pudding. Years later, Deschamps went to a restaurant and tried to order plum pudding, but they said they ran out and gave the last one to... Mr. de Fortgibu! Then, at a dinner party where they were serving plum pudding, Deschamps made a joke about Mr. de Fortgibu, and guess who showed up at the door? Yep, you guessed it! Mr. de Fortgibu was accidentally at the wrong party but still ended up at the right place at the right time. Each of the three times in life that they randomly met, a plum pudding was involved!

SURVIVING AGAINST THE ODDS

First, let's go back in time to the year 1914. Sir Ernest Shackleton, a fearless explorer, set off on a mission to be the first person to cross the continent of Antarctica on foot. But guess what? His ship got stuck in ice, leaving him and his crew stranded on a big chunk of ice in the middle of nowhere!

But Shackleton didn't give up. With a small group of brave crew members, he hopped into their largest lifeboat. They sailed a mind-boggling 800 miles, facing crazy challenges like icebergs, rough seas, and harsh weather. After reaching an island called South Georgia, Shackleton and two others climbed a huge mountain range to get help from a whaling station. And they succeeded! Every single stranded crew member was saved in the end.

IT'S IN OUR NATURE...

Imagine four brave children, ages 1, 4, 9, and 13, surviving a plane crash and being stranded in the Amazon rainforest for 40 days! These amazing kids were part of an indigenous community, and they used their cultural knowledge to find safe plants to eat until they were rescued. The whole country celebrated their incredible survival. What better motivation to learn what's edible in our surroundings?

We're travelling back to 1971 in Peru. Juliane Koepcke, a 17-year-old high school graduate, was on a plane with her mum to a remote biological station. Lightning struck the plane in mid-air, and it broke apart!

Amazingly, Juliane survived a fall of almost 10,000 feet while still strapped to her seat! Talk about a wild ride! After the crash, she spent 11 days all alone in the Peruvian rainforest. With a broken collarbone and a wounded arm, she battled insect bites and even had maggots crawling on her. Eww!

Finally, after searching for help, she found a logging camp where they gave her first aid. She was airlifted to a hospital and helped locate the bodies of the other victims, including her mum. Juliane's incredible story was even made into a documentary and a book!

It's time to jump into the deep sea off the coast of Nigeria in 2013. Imagine being a ship's cook named Harrison Okene, just minding your own business in the bathroom when suddenly, a powerful storm flips your tugboat upside down and sinks it!

Fortunately, Harrison managed to find a small air pocket inside the sunken boat, even though he was trapped underwater. He stayed there for more than two days in freezing water, running out of oxygen and getting really scared. But then, a group of awesome South African divers arrived and heard his faint hammering sounds. They found him and rescued him from the depths of the sea! Harrison was a true survivor, and even experts said it was a miracle that he made it.

Let's head for the skies with Vesna Vulović, a brave flight attendant. Her plane plummeted a whopping 10,000 metres (33,000 feet) from the sky! She was the only survivor, and doctors thought she'd be paralyzed forever, but guess what? Vesna defied the odds and was back on her feet in just ten months! What a survivor.

Timothy Shaddock decided to chase his dream of sailing solo across the ocean. The 54-year-old Australian left his business job and bought a 30-foot catamaran boat in Mexico. He trained in the Sea of Cortez, but when hurricane season approached, he set sail into the Pacific. While sailing under a full moon, he faced a storm that damaged his boat and left him stranded at sea for months.

During his challenging time at sea, Shaddock found strength through meditation, swimming, and journaling. His faithful companion, Bella, a black and brown stray dog he had met in Mexico, also kept him going. They survived on raw fish and rainwater.

Eventually, a helicopter pilot from a tuna boat spotted them 2,000 kilometres from land, and they were rescued. Bella's presence provided comfort and motivation for Shaddock to keep going during their ordeal. There's no doubt that dogs are incredible companions in hard situations!

We're in the scorching Sahara Desert in 1994. Mauro Prosperi, an incredible Olympic athlete, was competing in a race called the Marathon des Sables. But uh-oh, Mauro got lost and ended up spending a whole ten days in the vast desert! To survive, he had to drink his own urine (yuck!), eat raw lizards (gross!), and even drink the blood of bats (whoa!). Finally, Algerian police came to his rescue. It was much more of a challenge than he signed up for.

Let's join the Robertson family on their incredible sea adventure. In 1972, their ship was attacked and destroyed by killer whales! What are the chances? Stranded in a small lifeboat with their three children and a friend, they battled the elements of the wild ocean for 36 days until a Japanese fishing trawler rescued them. The family kept a journal during their ordeal, and their story was told in the book 'Survive the Savage Sea.'

Time to sail with Steven Callahan. He set off on a solo voyage across the Atlantic Ocean, but his ship sank in a storm. Can you picture being adrift in a small inflatable raft for 76 days? That's what Steven went through! With only a little food, water, and some gear, he drifted over 2,900 kilometres (1,800 miles) before reaching land and getting rescued. It took immense mental toughness to survive, and he even invented different characters in his mind, like a 'captain' and a 'crewman,' to help him stay strong.

We're off to Thailand in 2018. A group of boys who loved playing soccer and their coach went on an adventure into a cave. Out of nowhere, heavy rains flooded the cave, trapping them inside for two whole weeks! They had no food or water and were stuck deep underground.

It was a tough situation, but finally, after a immense rescue mission, divers found them and brought them back to safety. Thousands of people, including divers, rescue workers, and police helicopters, all came together to save the boys and their coach. They pumped out billions of litres of water from the cave! In the end, every single one of them was rescued and recovered from their gruelling 18-day adventure.

Abby Sunderland, a brave young sailor, wanted to become the youngest person to sail solo around the world, but a powerful storm damaged her boat and left her stranded in the ocean, 2,000 miles from land! Luckily, fishermen saw her signal and rescued her two days later.

BETWEEN A ROCK AND A HARD PLACE

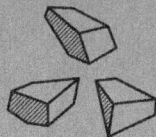

Aron Ralston, a mechanical engineer turned mountaineer, loved climbing mountains. In 2003, he embarked on a solo adventure to Canyonlands National Park in Utah. Aron was experienced and thought everything would be smooth sailing. But oh boy, was he in for a surprise!

~~~~~~~~~~~~~~~

As Aron descended into Bluejohn Canyon, a humongous rock slipped and trapped his right hand against the canyon wall with an 800-pound boulder. Ouch! Talk about being stuck between a rock and a hard place! To make things worse, Aron hadn't told anyone about his trip, so nobody knew he was in trouble.

For days, Aron survived on his limited food supply of two burritos and some candy bar crumbs. When that ran out, he had to resort to drinking his own urine. Eww, gross! He was getting weaker and feeling helpless, but then something amazing happened.

~~~~~~~~~~~~~~~

In a dream, Aron saw himself with an amputated arm playing with a child. He took it as a sign that he could survive. So, with sheer determination, he did something incredibly brave. He used the strength of his trapped arm to break his own bones, then used whatever he had – a water bottle tube, a knife, and pliers – to amputate his arm. Unimaginable! After the intense DIY surgery, Aron climbed out of the canyon, rappelled down a 20-metre (65-foot) cliff, and hiked for six miles until he came across a kind family who helped him and called for help. Phew!

Aron's story of survival became famous and even inspired a movie called '127 Hours.' But guess what? Even after such a terrifying experience, Aron didn't give up on his passion. In 2005, he became the first person to climb all 59 of Colorado's super-tall mountains.

YEARS ON A DESERT ISLAND

MEET ALEXANDER SELKIRK

This brave Scottish sailor who had some thrilling seafaring adventures. He sailed off to South America on a big adventure but ended up in a tough situation.

You see, Alexander didn't get along with his captain, Thomas Stradling, and they had a big fight. During a stop on a mysterious island, Alexander tried to rebel and stay on the shore, hoping the crew would support him. But Captain Stradling called his bluff and left Alexander all alone on the island. Oh no!

Being stranded didn't stop our adventurer, though. Alexander used his survival skills to make the best of the situation. He hunted lobsters and crawfish for food and even built his own shelter. He read passages from the Bible and sang songs to lift his spirits.

Four long years passed until Alexander's rescue! Finally, in 1709, a brave English privateer named Woodes Rogers came to the island and saved our stranded sailor. It was quite the daring rescue!
Alexander's incredible story inspired many books, including the famous novel Robinson Crusoe by Daniel Defoe. Alexander's real-life adventures became the blueprint for an amazing adventure tale.

Get ready for a long, challenging journey with Slavomir Rawicz. He was captured during a war and sent to a harsh labour camp in Siberia. But he didn't give up! In 1941, Slavomir and six other prisoners escaped. They marched 6,400 kilometres (4,000 miles) on foot, crossing frozen tundra, deserts, and even the mighty Himalayan Mountains to reach freedom.

Let's talk about Steve Fossett's lucky fall. In 2007, during his attempt to fly around the world solo in a balloon, he encountered a fierce storm over the Coral Sea off the coast of Australia. The storm destroyed his balloon, and Fossett's passenger capsule started plummeting to the ground. Miraculously, Fossett survived the fall without any harm and escaped from the sinking capsule. He was later rescued after 10 hours in the water.

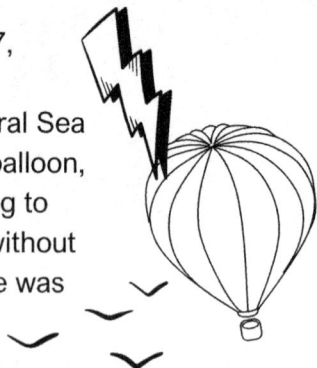

Now we have the amazing tale of Jose Salvador Alvarenga. He found himself lost at sea for a staggering 438 days! Can you imagine drifting in the Pacific Ocean for over a year? Jose's fishing trip took an unexpected turn, and he had to survive on his own. He caught birds, turtles, and fish for food and had to rely on his resourcefulness to stay alive until he washed up on a tiny Pacific island in 2013 and was rescued by some coconut farmers. He was nearly 11,000 kilometres (6,700 miles) from the place he had started!

MORE EXTRAORDINARY TALES AWAIT...

Here's the incredible story of the Lykov family. In 1936, fleeing religious persecution, they ventured into the Siberian wilderness with just a few belongings. For five decades, this family lived in isolation, surviving by hunting, farming, and making clothes from hemp. They faced harsh winters and near starvation, and tragically, the mother lost her life. It wasn't until 1978 that they were discovered, having spent their entire lives separated from the rest of humanity. That's 42 years of isolation! They must have had some incredible knowledge of natural resources to survive that long in such a harsh environment.

OUTBACK ORDEAL

Matthew Allen was a runaway who went missing for a long time. This rebellious teenager decided to run away from home, but he didn't anticipate the challenges that awaited him. For nine weeks, he was lost in the Australian Outback. When hikers finally discovered him, he was weak, disoriented, and had lost half his body weight. He survived by drinking creek water and was lucky to make it through a record-breaking heatwave.

GRANDMA'S FOOTSTEPS

Let's follow Grandma Ann Rodger's wild journey down the wrong road. One day in 2016, Ann took a few wrong turns and ended up on a remote road in Tucson, Arizona. She ran out of fuel and her mobile phone didn't work. With her survival skills and resourcefulness, she managed to survive for nine days! Ann stayed in her car at night for warmth, built fires, and found food and water from the desert. She even roasted and ate a turtle! Finally, she made a huge 'help' sign and was rescued. Her loyal dog, Queenie, stuck by her side through it all.

This one's a strange tale of self-enforced survival. After the Second World War ended, Lieutenant Hiroo Onoda continued fighting in the Philippines, refusing to believe the war was over. He spent almost 30 years hiding in the jungle and avoiding capture. It wasn't until 1974, when he received orders from his former commanding officer, that he finally surrendered and emerged from the jungle.

Now, we have Tony Streather and John Emery, two adventurers who in 1957 faced extreme challenges while trying to summit Haramosh Peak in Pakistan. Despite avalanches, falls, and harsh weather, they were the only survivors out of the original group of four. They couldn't explain how they made it, but Tony felt like a mysterious being guided him, while John had an out-of-body experience.

Next, we have Anna Bågenholm, who has an incredible survival story. In 1999, after a skiing accident, she became trapped under a layer of ice in freezing water for 80 minutes. Her body temperature dropped to 13.7°C (56.7°F), the lowest ever recorded in a human, but she found an air pocket and survived against all odds.

This is Peter Skyllberg's chilling tale of being buried alive in Sweden. In the winter of 2011, Peter's car got stuck in the snow, and he was trapped inside for a mind-boggling 60 days! He survived by living off the snow and researchers believe his body went into a type of hibernation to help him save his energy and survive. The snow that piled on top of this car will also have helped to protect him from the chilling -30C air outside. It's enough to make you shiver!

Let's sail through stormy waters with **Tami Ashcraft**, who truly kept her head in a crisis. She found herself in a life-or-death situation when a storm hit while she was sailing with her fiancé and friends in the Pacific Ocean. Their boat got damaged, and they were left drifting in the vast ocean. But Tami didn't lose hope. She took charge and used her limited knowledge of navigation to plot a course towards Hawaii, thousands of miles away. For a whopping 41 days, she and her friends faced hunger, thirst, and exhaustion, but they never gave up. Tami's incredible journey later inspired people around the world when she wrote a book about her experience called 'Red Sky in Mourning.'

VOLCANIC ACTIVITY

Imagine being stuck in the mouth of a big volcano! Chris Duddy, Michael Benson and Craig Hosking know how that feels. They were inside a helicopter, filming a volcano called Kilauea in Hawaii when they crashed into the crater!

But luck hadn't abandoned them completely. The helicopter missed landing in boiling lava by a hair, and all three of them got away with just small cuts. The volcano spews very toxic gases, but fortunately, they found a spot in the crater where there was some fresh air from the top. Then Craig, the pilot, radioed for help and managed to get out of there, but Chris and Michael were stuck because the rescuer couldn't find them in all the smoke and the volcano walls kept falling apart as they tried to climb up.

Chris finally managed to climb out, and he made it to safety after 27 long hours. Michael stayed behind, worried about his buddies, unsure that they were alive. He held on, praying and even talking to the volcano goddess, Pele. He said, 'You're not taking me!' And guess what? On Monday morning, a helicopter pilot named Tom Hauptman spotted Michael through the steam and rescued him. He made it out okay and told the volcano, 'You didn't beat me!' I bet they never imagined that this volcano-filming trip would be crazy enough to create the plot for its own film!

Howard Ulrich's boat was carried by a massive wave while fishing with his son in 1958. A gigantic wave caused by an earthquake swept them up in Lituya Bay, Alaska. The earthquake was a massive 7.8 on the Richter scale. Can you believe they were carried at an astonishing speed of 161 kilometres per hour (100 miles per hour)? The wave lifted them over trees and then gently placed them back down onto the bay. They must have thanked their lucky stars for such an unlikely survival.

In 1979, 11-year-old Norman Ollestad found himself in a plane crash on a mountain in California, US. With his father tragically gone, he had to navigate the treacherous terrain carrying his father's partner Sandra who was terribly injured. He made a courageous descent. Unfortunately, Sandra couldn't continue, and he had to leave her behind. After nine hours, he found help and survived to share his incredible story.

Meet the brave crew of Apollo 13. In 1970, they set out to reach the moon but faced a dangerous situation when an oxygen tank exploded, damaging their spacecraft. They had to think fast and use the lunar module to make it back to Earth. With limited food and facing dehydration, they managed to slingshot around the moon and safely return home. It was a miracle landing!

Now let's hear about Reshma Begum's incredible survival after a building collapse. In 2013, Reshma was working as a seamstress in Bangladesh when the building she was in collapsed, trapping her underneath for a shocking 17 days. She managed to find some food and water to stay alive until rescuers heard her cries for help. She was reunited with her family, safe and sound.

Matt Suter had a wild encounter with a twister in 2006. While inside his grandma's trailer home in Missouri, US, he was swept up by a powerful tornado. Miraculously, he survived being thrown the length of several football fields with only minor bruises and cuts. Funnily enough, it's not that far from Kansas, where fictional character Dorothy also had her home swept up by a tornado in 'The Wizard of Oz'.

SPORTING TRIUMPHS

Gail Devers' Tough Journey: Gail Devers was a sprinter and hurdler, and she was awesome! But she got really ill with something called Grave's disease. She couldn't walk and doctors thought about amputating her feet. Luckily, she recovered, and in 1991, she won a silver medal at the World Championships. Then, she won heaps more gold medals in the Olympics and World Championships. Talk about a comeback!

Roger Bannister's Epic Mile Run: Here is a classic sports moment from 1954 in Oxford, UK. This was a time when experts said that running a mile in under four minutes was impossible! Well, Roger Bannister didn't listen to those experts. He trained mega hard and pushed himself to the limit.

On the big day, it was cold, the track was wet, and there weren't many people watching. But Roger ran the 1.6 kilometres (one mile) in just three minutes and fifty-nine seconds! After Roger did it, other runners also started breaking that record. It's like he opened the door to possibility!

Michael van Gerwen's Near-Perfect Darts: Do you think you have a good aim? Well, in 2018 in London, England, Michael van Gerwen did something almost impossible. He threw 17 perfect darts in a row during a darts game! He was so close to hitting all the bullseyes and getting a '9-darter' twice in a row, which is super hard to do. It's like getting two hole-in-ones in golf one after the other!

Alex Honnold's Daredevil Climb: Now, imagine climbing a 900-metre (3,000-feet) tall cliff face without any safety gear. That's what Alex Honnold did in 2016 in California, US. People call it 'free soloing,' and it's super dangerous because there's nothing to catch you if you fall. Alex climbed a place called El Capitán in less than four hours! Some folks even compare it to landing on the moon because it's so incredible!

160

FAST OR SLOW?

Conor McGregor's Lightning KO: In 2015 in Las Vegas, USA, there was a fighter named Jose Aldo who hadn't lost a fight in over ten years! He was a big deal in the world of UFC. Conor McGregor was his opponent. Conor had already won another championship, and people couldn't wait to see these two fighters in the ring. When the fight finally happened, it was over in just 14 seconds! Conor threw a punch, and bam! He knocked out Jose Aldo. That's one speedy victory.

The Never-Ending Tennis Match: Now, let's talk about tennis in 2010 at Wimbledon, UK. John Isner and Nicholas Mahut played a tennis match that lasted for three days! They served the ball over 100 times each! Finally, John Isner won, but it was one of the most intense tennis matches ever. Just the final set was longer than most entire matches!

Muhammad Ali's Amazing Brilliant Boxing: In 1966, the boxing legend faced a massive problem. He didn't want to go to the Vietnam war, because he didn't believe the fighting could bring peace. So he said no, and that got him in trouble. They took away his boxing licence in many places in the US, and he was only 24 years old!

He couldn't box at the big leagues for five whole years, until 1971. When he finally came back, he had a super tough fight against Joe Frazier, and he lost. But guess what? Three years later, he fought against Joe Foreman in something called the 'Rumble in the Jungle,' and he won! He stood up for what he believed in and reclaimed his status as world heavyweight champion.

Monica Seles' Tennis Comeback: Now, imagine you're a tennis star, and while you're playing in a tournament, someone stabs you in the back! It happened in 1993. But even though she had deep scars and got seriously hurt, she didn't give up on tennis. She took a break for two years, and when she came back, guess what she did? She won the Australian Open in 1996 and added more big tennis trophies to her collection.

Sydney Wooderson's Running Triumph: Sydney Wooderson was a tiny guy with big dreams. In the 1930s, he was performing really well but missed the Olympics because of an ankle injury. But Sydney didn't see it as the end of his sporting career. He set new world records and won a European championship! Then, the Second World War came, and Sydney couldn't go to the Olympics again. He became a firefighter but got sick with a serious fever that left him in hospital for several months. Guess what? He recovered (again!) and won another championship in 1946.

JOY FOR THE JUNIORS...

Mike Tyson Becomes a Champion at 20: Now, let's talk about 'Iron' Tyson. In 1986 in Las Vegas, USA, Tyson became the youngest Heavyweight Boxing Champion in the world when he was just 20 years old! He defeated the champion at the time, Trevor Berbick, in just five minutes and 35 seconds. Tyson was lightning-fast and super strong. It's like winning the biggest championship when you're just out of school!

Chloe Kim's Astonishing Award: Heard of this famous American snowboarder? When she was only 17, she won a gold medal in the Winter Olympics for snowboarding, and she was the youngest woman ever to do that. It's a long sporting career when you start winning as a teenager!

Bethany Hamilton's Surfing Success:
Imagine you're 13, and you love surfing, but then a shark bites off your whole left arm! That's what happened to Bethany Hamilton. It was super scary, and she lost a lot of blood. But here's the amazing part: Bethany didn't give up on her dream to be a pro surfer. She came back to surfing with a special longer board that she could use with one arm. And she didn't just come back; she started winning surf competitions! Her story was so inspiring that she even wrote a book about it, and it became a bestseller.

MORE CHAMPIONS...

Betty Robinson's Olympic Comeback: Meet Betty Robinson, the speedy queen! She became an Olympic champion when she was just 16! She was as fast as the wind and even broke a world record.

But then, something terrible happened. In 1931, Betty was in a plane crash and was seriously injured. She was in a wheelchair and couldn't run for a long time. But that wasn't the end of her sporting career! She worked super hard and joined a relay team at the Olympics. They won, and against all the odds, Betty got her second gold medal!

Glory Alozie and Carolin Schäfer's Heartfelt Silvers: Glory Alozie and her fiancé were excited to go to the Olympics in 2000. But her fiancé had a car accident and passed away. Glory was devastated, but she still went to the Olympics. She ran like the wind and won a silver medal, even though it was tough for her. Glory said, 'This medal is very important to me, the most important in my life.'

Carolin Schäfer suffered a similar tragedy when her boyfriend passed away. She is a heptathlete, which means she competes at seven different events to earn a medal. After the accident, she tried her best but couldn't finish a competition. Two years later in 2017, she performed incredibly and won a silver medal at the World Championships. It meant a lot to her.

Ronnie O'Sullivan's Super Snooker: Let's talk about snooker, a game with colourful balls and a long table. The toughest thing to do in snooker is to score a maximum, which is 147 points. Ronnie O'Sullivan did something amazing in 1997 in Sheffield, UK. He scored a maximum break in just five minutes and eight seconds! That's like clearing the table super fast, taking less than nine seconds per shot! Ronnie got a huge prize of £147,000.

Eliud Kipchoge's Marvellous Marathon: In 2019, in Vienna, Austria, Eliud Kipchoge ran a whole marathon, that's 42.2 kilometres (26.2 miles), in under two hours! Before that, people said it couldn't be done. Eliud finished in 1 hour, 59 minutes, and 40 seconds. He said, 'This shows no one is limited.' It means you can do anything if you try hard enough!

COME BACK BETTER

Fabrice Muamba's Miraculous Victory: Sometimes, sports stories are not just about skill and winning. They're also about incredible comebacks. In 2012, something amazing happened in London, England. During a soccer game between Bolton Wanderers and Tottenham Hotspur, Fabrice Muamba suddenly collapsed on the field.

It turned out he had a serious heart problem. It was really scary because it seemed like he was gone for 78 minutes! His heart stopped, but the doctors kept trying. They shocked his heart 15 times, and he came back to life! He had to retire from playing soccer, but he's grateful to be alive.

Bob Champion and Aldaniti's Grand National Win: In 1981, something cool happened at the Grand National, a famous horse race. Jockey Bob Champion and his horse Aldaniti won, but it was more than just a race. Bob Champion got cancer in 1979 when he was only 31 years old. And his horse, Aldaniti, had some serious leg problems. People thought they might have to put the horse down! But their fates dramatically changed. In 1981, they won the UK Grand National! Their story was so heartwarming that they even got named Team of the Year at the BBC Sports Awards. His name says it all: Champion.

Ana Quirot's Brave Comeback: This amazing runner from Cuba won lots of races and set records. But one day in 1993, she suffered serious burns after a flammable liquid in her kitchen exploded. She even lost her unborn baby. Ana's brave response was, 'I'm going to run again!' After lots of surgery she came back to win a world title and medals in the Olympics!

Paul Pierce's Basketball Triumph: In 2000, something terrible happened to Paul Pierce, nicknamed 'The Truth.' He got stabbed 11 times in the neck, face, and back during a fight at a nightclub! It was super tough, and he had depression because of it.

But he didn't stop playing basketball. In fact, he won an NBA championship with the Boston Celtics in 2008 and was picked for the All-Star team ten times! And here's the incredible part: He's not just playing basketball; he's also helping raise money for the hospital that helped him and for people who have depression. What a hero!

Jesse Owens' Awesome Olympics: In 1936, a speedy guy named Jesse Owens rocked the world. Before the Olympics, he set three world records in just one hour! It's a feat that's never been equalled.

But there was a twist. Some people didn't want Jesse to go to the Olympics because it was taking place in Berlin, Germany just before the Second World War, and Hilter was overseeing it.

Jesse wasn't deterred by the racism some said he would face for being black in a country led by a man who believed in white supremacy. He went to the Olympics and won four gold medals in running and jumping. What an incredible act of defiance!

Ben Hogan's Unbelievable Golf Comeback: There was this golf superstar named Ben Hogan. He won a bunch of big golf tournaments, but then something crazy happened. When he was just 36 he got into a really bad car crash, when his car hit a big bus. Ben Hogan had lots of broken bones and even blood clots, and he had to stay in the hospital for nearly two months. But here's the jaw-dropping part: just 18 months later, he won the US Open! He was tired, but he still won five out of six tournaments in 1953, including big ones like the US Open and the British Open. Some people are unstoppable!

Hermann Maier's Surprising Skiing:
Meet 'The Hermanator,' one of the best skiers ever. But he had a big accident on his motorcycle in 2001, and doctors thought they might have to cut off his leg! Instead, they did a lot of surgery to fix his leg. Lots of people thought he couldn't ski anymore. But he proved them all wrong! He came back and won more big skiing titles, like the World Cup and the World Championship.

Niki Lauda's Fiery Return to Formula 1:
Niki Lauda, a famous Formula 1 driver, won his first championship in 1975. But the following year his Ferrari car burst into flames during a terrifying race in Germany! He got badly burned and even almost died because he breathed in smoke. But guess what? Just a few weeks later, he was back on the racetrack! And not just that, he won the championship again in 1977 and even in 1984. That's some real courage right there!

Jonjo O'Neill's Horse Racing Resilience: Jonjo O'Neill was a jockey, and he had some tough times. First, he had two really bad accidents while riding horses, that were so bad that they thought he might lose his leg. Twice. Then, things got even harder. He had to fight cancer for two whole years! But you know what's amazing? Jonjo came back and won a big horse race called the Gold Cup on a horse named Dawn Run in 1986! He became a trainer after that and won more races at a famous place called Cheltenham, UK. He even won the Grand National in 2010 with a horse called Don't Push It. Talk about being tough!

MESSAGE IN A BOTTLE

It's a romantic image we all recognise from stories … a message in a bottle washes up on the shore with a life-changing message inside. Here are some cases where that truly happened. Despite the joy these bottles have brought people, with our seas and oceans already full of rubbish, we should stick to more eco-friendly ways of communicating!

Transatlantic Pen Pals: A long time ago, in 1945, a man named Frank sent a bottle with a message into the sea. An 18-year-old milkmaid named Breda found it in Ireland. They wrote letters for seven years and finally met in 1952. A lot of people hoped they would marry, and the newspapers got excited. However, they decided to stay friends, like a pen pal connection across the ocean.

An Unfinished Story: A long time ago in 1915, the ship Lusitania was hit by a torpedo and quickly sank. A passenger wrote a note and shoved it into a bottle in the last moments but ran out of time before he could finish it properly. The note read: 'Still on deck with a few people. The last boats have left. We are sinking fast. Some men near me are praying with a priest. The end is near. Maybe this note will… ' We'll never know how it ends.

A Message of Escape: In 1979, during a cruise to Hawaii, Dorothy and John wrote messages in bottles and put money inside, so whoever found them could afford to send them a letter in return. Several years later, they received a response from a man named Hoa Van Nguyen, who was trying to escape from Vietnam. They kept in touch via letters, and in 1985 with the help of Dorothy and John, Hoa and his family managed to move to the US and they finally met up in person. That message changed lives.

Zoe's Ocean Note: Picture a 10-year-old girl named Zoe, who wrote a sweet message and put it in a bottle during a ferry ride. She liked ballet, and playing the flute, and had a hamster named Sparkle and a fish called Speckle. After 23 years, her message was found by a couple in the Netherlands and sent back to her. It's like a letter that travelled through time.

A Message from Castaways: A long time ago, in 1794, a Japanese sailor named Chunosuke Matsuyama and his shipmates faced a big storm and got shipwrecked on a remote island. Matsuyama carved a message into a piece of coconut wood and put it in a bottle to see if they could get help. After 150 years, the bottle reached a village in Japan. It told the sad story of the castaways and finally solved the mystery of what happened to them.

FROM BOY TO MAN

A Boy's Message: In 2011, a 13-year-old boy from Russia found a bottle with a note inside. The note was in German and was from a 5-year-old named Frank. By the time the note was discovered Frank was 29. The two met in an online call, creating a unique connection across time and seas.

A Surprising Letter from the Sea: It started with a simple brown bottle, found by a fisherman in the Baltic Sea. Over a hundred years ago, a man named Richard Platz tossed this bottle into the sea during a hike along the German coast. He had no idea it would take 101 years for his message to reach its destination. In 1946, he passed away, never getting the chance to meet his granddaughter, Angela Erdmann. However, a determined investigator followed the clues and eventually reached Angela's doorstep with a postcard from her long-lost grandfather.

Love in a Bottle: In 1956, a long time before online dating, a lonely sailor from Sweden put a message in a bottle and threw it into the sea. The message began 'To Someone Beautiful and Far Away'. A lady from Sicily found it two years later and sent a sweet reply: 'I am not beautiful, but it seems so miraculous that this little bottle should have travelled so far and long to reach me that I must send you an answer.' They ended up writing a lot of letters and falling in love, and he moved to Sicily to marry his match made by the sea.

A Grandson's Discovery: Imagine finding a bottle with a note from 1936! Geoff found one on a New Zealand beach. The note asked the finder to send it to an address in Australia. After some detective work, they found the grandson of the person who sent the message, who was pleased to feel a connection with his long-lost grandfather. It's like a bottle connecting different generations and places.

A Lifesaving Message: In 2005 more than 80 young people were stranded on a boat near Costa Rica and with no way of communicating with land. They put an SOS message in a bottle, and amazingly a fisherman found it and alerted the authorities on an island nearby, who quickly rescued them. Thanks to this message, they were saved.

A Texas Treasure Hunt: Jim and Candy Duke found a special bottle tangled in tree branches on a Texas beach. Inside was a postcard with instructions from the past, asking them to fill out a form and send it back to the laboratory. It turned out this bottle was part of an old science experiment in 1962 to study how shrimps move with ocean currents. They sent the postcard back but said no thanks to the 50-cent reward.

A Titanic Message: In 1912 two cousins, Jeremiah and Nora, were on the Titanic. Just before the ship sank, Jeremiah put a message saying 'From Titanic, goodbye all. Burke of Glanmire, Cork', in a holy water bottle that his mother had given him. Strangely, it was found in Ireland a year later not far from where their family lived. The bottle stayed in the family for almost 100 years before it went to a museum.

A Message to Remember: In the early 2000s a 10-year-old girl called Sidonie wrote a message in a bottle while visiting friends in New York, and it floated away. Later, after a huge storm in 2012, the bottle was found in a park. What makes this discovery special is that the girl had already passed away two years earlier after falling off a cliff in Switzerland, and the message she had left was a reminder to be kind.

A Bottle's Epic Journey: Think about this: a kid named Max wrote a message including his name, address and interests, sealed it in a bottle, and threw it into the ocean when he was just 10. Nine years later, while he was at university, he got a text from his dad with a big surprise. The bottle had travelled all the way from Massachusetts to France! It's like a message that went on a 6000-kilometre world tour.

A Mother's Sad Message: A long time ago, a mother threw a special bottle into the sea with a letter inside. She was so sad because her son, Maurice, had died aged 13. She wrote about how much she missed him. The bottle was found by a dog walker on a beach in England, and it held a lock of hair. A friend, who was an author called Karen, translated the letter and tried hard to find the French mother but with no luck. In 2006, Karen wrote a book called 'The Letter in the Bottle' inspired by this mystery. A few years later the French mother wrote to the author after seeing the book, and they finally met up in France, bringing the mystery to a close.

Jonathan's Mysterious Message: A young kite surfer named Matea found one while cleaning a beach in Croatia. It was from someone named Jonathan all the way in Canada, 6000 kilometres across the ocean. The note was 28 years old and just said, 'Mary, you really are a great person. I hope we can keep in correspondence. Your friend always, Jonathan, Nova Scotia, 1985.' But who were Mary and Jonathan? That's still a mystery!

BIG SKY

Get ready to be wowed by the most mind-blowing wonders that Mother Nature has up her sleeve. You won't believe the incredible stuff she's been hiding right under our noses. From sparkling gems to electrifying storms and everything in between, we're about to embark on a wild ride through the world of natural marvels.

WACKY WEATHER

Fallstreak Holes: Sometimes, clouds have holes in them that look like perfect circles or ovals. These gaps are created when part of the cloud freezes and falls, leaving a hole behind.

Brocken Spectre: Have you ever seen a rainbow around your shadow on a cloud? It looks like a magical halo! This cool trick happens when the sun is behind you, and your shadow is cast onto a cloud or fog, so you have to be pretty high up to have a chance of seeing it.

Ball Lightning: Imagine you're in a thunderstorm, and suddenly, you see a glowing ball in the sky, about the size of a basketball. That's what ball lightning is! Scientists are still trying to figure out how it forms because it's so unpredictable.

Northern Lights (Aurora Borealis): Way up near the North Pole, there's a magical light show in the sky! It's caused by sunlight particles from the sun bumping into our air and making colourful lights. You can see green, red, and purple lights, depending on where and how it happens. The best time to catch the northern lights is in winter when it's dark, far away from city lights, and the sky is clear.

Morning Glory Clouds: Down in Australia, sometimes they have these long, tube-shaped clouds that look like waves in the sky. It's a mesmerising pattern made by nature.

Mammatus Clouds: If clouds could look like cotton balls or bubbles, that's what Mammatus clouds would be. They hang down from other clouds and often appear before or after big thunderstorms.

Lava Tornadoes: During volcanic eruptions, something crazy happens – lava turns into tornado-like spirals! These fire whirls are a reminder of how powerful volcanoes can be.

Rainbows: They happen when sunlight bounces around inside raindrops, creating a beautiful arch of colours. Remember, you'll always see a rainbow opposite the sun in the sky. If you're looking at the sun, the rainbow will be behind you. Sometimes, if light bounces inside a raindrop twice, you might even spot a second, fainter rainbow above the first one!

Waterspouts: Think of a tornado over the water – that's a waterspout! They can be harmless or dangerous, but they're always a swirling column connecting the ocean to the clouds.

Dust Devils: Picture a tiny tornado made of dust and debris dancing around on a hot, sunny day. Dust devils might not be dangerous, but they're fascinating to watch as they spin across the ground.

Lenticular Clouds: Imagine being near a mountain and seeing clouds that look like flying saucers stacked on top of each other. These are lenticular clouds, formed by air flowing over the mountain.

WEATHER WARNING

Now let's talk about places that know how to make a splash!
Mawsynram in India takes the prize for the highest average annual rainfall. Over 10 years, it received a mind-blowing 11,872 millimetres (467 inches) of rain. Imagine how many swimming pools you could fill with that...

In one minute, Barot in Guadeloupe, France experienced a whopping 38 millimetres (1.5 inches) of rain. It poured down from 11:03 to 11:04am on 26 November 1970. That's like an afternoon of heavy rain falling in just 60 seconds!

INSANE RAIN

In Cilaos, Réunion, things got soaking wet in just 24 hours. During Tropical Cyclone Denise on 7–8 January 1966, a staggering 1,825 millimetres (72 inches) of rain fell. Many places that are considered to be relatively rainy don't get that much water in a year!

But not all places receive lots of rain. In Quillagua, Chile, the annual rainfall is a mere 0.2 millimetres (0.008 inches) or even less.

And if you think rain only lasts a few days, think again. Oahu in Hawaii holds the record for the most consecutive days with measurable rain. For a whopping 331 days, it rained at least 0.25 millimetres (0.01 inches) each day. The song 'Why does it always rain on me?' has never been more appropriate. If you include any tiny trace of rain at all, Oahu's record goes up to 881 days straight! That's over 2 years!

174

MIND-BLOWING WIND...

Imagine a wind so strong it could knock you off your feet! In the Bridge Creek-Moore tornado on 3 May 1999, near Oklahoma City and Moore, US, the wind reached an unimaginable speed of 484 kilometres per hour (301 miles per hour) in just a 3-second gust. That's like the wind competing with the fastest racing cars on Earth!

Imagine hailstones as heavy as a big bag of sugar. In Bangladesh, 1986, the heaviest hailstone ever recorded weighed a kilogram (two pounds). And in South Dakota, a new size record was set in 2010. The hailstones reached 20 centimetres in diameter. You wouldn't want one of those landing on your head!

SNOW WOW

Enjoy waking up in a winter wonderland? On 14 February 1927, Mount Ibuki in Japan got a mind-blowing 230 centimetres (7.5 feet) of snow in just 24 hours. You could build a whole snow town with that.

But the snowfall didn't stop there. In Tamarack, California, the snow piled up like crazy. In January 1911, a whopping 9.9 metres (32.5 feet) of snow fell in just one month. That's taller than a three-storey building! By March, the snow depth reached a mind-boggling 11.5 metres (37.7 feet), the greatest ever recorded in North America.

SUN POWER

On 29 December 2003, at Licancabur volcano on the Chilean-Bolivian border, the ultraviolet index reached an incredibly high value of 43 (a typical hot summer's day might be UV Index 9). In such conditions, someone with light skin can get a moderate sunburn in just four minutes!

CATATUMBO LIGHTNING

Lake Maracaibo is a massive body of water in Venezuela that connects to the Caribbean Sea through the Tablazo Strait. It's not just any lake; it's a brackish tidal estuary, which means it's a mix of fresh and salty water. This place is HUGE, covering an area of about 13,200 square kilometres (5,100 square miles). It was the biggest lake in all of South America at one point!

But what makes Lake Maracaibo super famous is the incredible weather event called Catatumbo lightning. This is a special kind of lightning that happens here more than anywhere else in the world. It's like a never-ending light show in the sky!

The Catatumbo lightning is born when warm air from Lake Maracaibo meets the cold air from the Andes mountains. When these two air masses clash, it creates these fantastic lightning storms. This amazing lightning show happens about 160 nights every year, and when it does, it's intense.

The lake gets over 280 lightning strikes every hour, and this lasts for about 10 hours each day. That's a lot of lightning!

STRIKING LIGHTNING

Did you know that lightning can travel mega long distances?
The longest lightning bolt ever recorded stretched an incredible 768 kilometres (477 miles) across the southern US on 29 April 2020. That's as wide as the whole of Germany!

It can also last for a while. The longest duration for a single lightning flash was a mind-boggling 17.1 seconds on 18 June 2020, in Uruguay and northern Argentina. You could blink seven times and it would probably still be there!

Red lightning is not your everyday lightning bolt. You don't see it all the time, and it's a bit tricky to spot or record. To witness these special red lightning flashes, you need just the right conditions, like a clear view with no other lights around. Here's the thing, though. Red lightning isn't usually all that strong, and it doesn't stick around for very long, usually just a couple of seconds. So, it's not considered especially dangerous. But it has been linked to some strange aeroplane accidents that have occurred above thunderstorms. So, while it might not be dangerous on the ground, it can be a bit risky up in the skies.

WHAT A STAR!

Distant Stars: You know those tiny sparkling dots in the night sky? Well, most of them are very, very far away. Some are so far that the light we see from them started its journey millions of years ago! When you see that light you're seeing a star's past.

Earth's next-door neighbour is a star called Alpha Centauri. But here's the thing: it's over four light-years away! That means the light we see from Alpha Centauri left there more than four years ago. That's a long cosmic journey!

Star Variety: Stars aren't all the same. Some are like superstars – big and super hot, way hotter than our sun! Others are like dying fires – smaller and cooler. And it's like a celestial rainbow because they come in different colours too, depending on how hot they are.

Supernova Show: When a really big star gets old, it can go out with a bang, a gigantic explosion called a supernova. These supernovae can shine super bright, even brighter than whole galaxies for a short time. Plus, they create new space stuff that makes the universe a lot more interesting!

PECULIAR

PLACES

Prepare to embark on a wild journey as we uncover the universe's weirdest, funniest, most remote, and mysteriously abandoned locations. Every corner holds a tale that will tickle your imagination and baffle your senses.

FUNNIEST PLACE NAMES

Accident, Maryland, US. Here people are called 'accidentals.'

Baby, Poland. This is a popular place name in Poland!

Bat Cave, North Carolina, US

Batman, Turkey. The mayor once threatened to sue the makers of the Dark Knight film trilogy. He wanted to be the only Batman! It turned out to be a publicity stunt, but it definitely put Batman on the map.

Beer, England

Bigfoot, Texas, US. You might expect a lot of sightings of Bigfoot there, but the name actually comes from Texas Ranger William A. A. 'Bigfoot' Wallace.

Boring, three different places in Oregon, Maryland and Tennessee, US

Buttzville, New Jersey

Catbrain, England. It should be twinned with Katzenhirn, Germany, which means the same thing!

Cheesequake, New Jersey, US

Choccolocco, Alabama, US. This town in Alabama, had a mysterious monster scare in the early 2000s. People kept seeing 'The Choccolocco Monster' at the edge of the woods, but it turned out to be a local teen dressed up in a cow's skull.

Christmas Pie, England

Cool, California, US

Ding Dong, Texas, US

Disappointment Islands, French Polynesia

Dum Dum, Kolkata, India

Dummer, New Hampshire, US.

Egg, Austria

Elephant Butte, New Mexico, US

Embarrass, Minnesota, US. It got its name from French fur traders who called the river 'Rivière d'Embarras,' meaning 'river of obstacles.'

Fail, Portugal. There's also a Failsworth in England

Fussy, France

Half.com, Oregon, US. This small town changed its name for a year to receive lots of money and computers for its schools.

Inexpressible Island, off the southern tip of Antarctica. It's so indescribable that it's simply called 'inexpressible.' It must be truly extraordinary!

Hell, Norway

Lost in Aberdeenshire, Scotland. This tiny hamlet is known for something unusual. People keep stealing their street signs! They might protest, but the name comes from the Gaelic word for inn.

Nameless, Tennessee, US. This town has an interesting story behind its name. Legend has it that the residents left a blank space on a form for a post office, so the government gave it the name 'Nameless.' Others say it was a protest when a Confederate general's name was rejected.

Normal, Illinois, US. The name comes from a school called Illinois State Normal

Pity Me, England

Peculiar, Missouri, US. When the people were trying to come up with a name for their town, they realised all the good ones were already taken. So, they settled on 'Peculiar' because they thought it was too strange to be duplicated. Now it has a fun slogan: 'Where the Odds Are With You.'

Poo, India

Random Lake, Wisconsin, US

Rottenegg, Austria

Rough and Ready, California. This town used to be a Gold Rush town. It got its name from a mining company named after President Zachary Taylor, who had a nickname: 'Old Rough and Ready.'

Scratchy Bottom, Dorset, England

Smug, Poland

Ugley, Essex, England. It's named after someone called 'Ugga'

University, which doesn't sound like a very interesting place to study!

Why, Arizona, US

Whynot, North Carolina, US

Zzyzx, California, US. This tiny place in the Mojave Desert used to be called Soda Springs, but a clever entrepreneur changed it to Zzyzx to make it memorable.

HA HA

HOT, HOT, HOT

• • • • • • • • • • • •

Death Valley, California: Imagine a place so hot it feels like stepping into an oven! Death Valley holds the record for the hottest air temperature ever recorded. In 1913, it reached a scorching 57°C (134°F) degrees Celsius! Ouch! Even today, normal summer temperatures in Death Valley reach a sizzling 47°C (117°F).

Dasht-e Loot, Iran: Brace yourselves for the hottest ground temperature ever measured! In this desert plateau, the ground can reach an incredible 70.7°C (159.3°F)! No wonder this place is uninhabited.

Dhahran, Saudi Arabia: The heat index combines air temperature and humidity. Dhahran holds the record for the highest heat index ever recorded. In July 2003, with an air temperature of 42°C (108°F), the heat index was 81°C (178°F). That's like literally living in a sauna.

OUT IN THE COLD

Verkhoyansk, Russia: Welcome to the land of extreme temperature swings! This Russian town within the Arctic Circle is known as the 'Pole of Cold.' In February 1892, it reached a mind-numbing -67.8°C (-90.0°F)! But here's the twist: Verkhoyansk also experiences surprisingly hot summers, with temperatures soaring above 30°C (86°F)! That's like going from Antarctica to the Sahara Desert in the same spot.

In Loma, Montana, in 1972, the temperature rose an incredible 57°C (103°F) in just one day! It went from a teeth-chattering -48°C (-54°F) to a relatively mild 9°C (49°F). That's like going from the icy Arctic to a spring afternoon in no time!

Oymyakon, Russia: Picture a place where even polar bears would need scarves! Oymyakon holds the title of one of the coldest permanently inhabited settlements on Earth. In February 1933, the temperature dropped to a bone-chilling -67.7°C (-89.9°F)! It's normally so cold that local schools only close when it dips below -52°C (-62°F). Brrr!

Dome Fuji, Antarctic: Brace yourself for the coldest place on Earth! In August 2010, the temperature at Dome Fuji in Antarctica plunged to a bone-chilling -93.2°C (-135.8°F)! This frozen desert is a window into the paleo-climatic history of our planet, with ice cores telling tales of the past 720,000 years. If you ever visit, be sure to pack a Thermos filled with hot cocoa to keep you warm!

RAPID CITY

Get ready for the fastest temperature drop you can imagine. In Rapid City (haha), South Dakota, on 10 January 1911, the temperature plunged a whopping 26°C (47°F) in just fifteen minutes! That's faster than you can drink a cup of tea. I bet a lot of people were wishing they'd brought their coats!

EXTREMES OF THE UNIVERSE

Hottest Place: Imagine a sizzling star that's like a cosmic oven... introducing the star at the centre of the Red Spider Nebula!

This scorching star is a real hotshot, with temperatures ranging from a toasty 150,000 to a mind-blowing 250,000 degrees Kelvin (that's roughly 249,726°C or 449,539°F). It's so blazing that it's hard for scientists to measure its exact temperature because it's hiding behind a thick dust shell. Talk about being on fire!

NASA has crowned this star as one of the hottest-known out there.

GET READY TO CHILL OUT, SPACE EXPLORER!

We're about to journey to the coldest place in the universe – the Boomerang Nebula, also known as the Bow Tie Nebula. It's located a whopping 5,000 light-years away in the Centaurus constellation. The Boomerang Nebula is a super cool cloud of dust and ionised gases. Imagine a cosmic snowstorm! At its centre is a dying red giant star, which used to shine brightly like our own sun. But as it nears the end of its life, it's shedding its outer layers, creating this beautiful nebula. What's mind-blowing is that the Boomerang Nebula is losing its mass a staggering 100 times faster than other dying stars. This rapid weight loss makes it the chilliest object ever discovered in the universe.

ABANDONED PLACES

The city of Neapolis in Tunisia was once a big and important Roman city, but a huge tsunami destroyed it a long time ago. Everyone thought it was lost forever until some cool archaeologists found it again in 2017. Imagine discovering a whole city buried under the ground! That is some pretty special hidden treasure.

There's a village called Vilarinho da Furna in Portugal that had a special democratic system. Every family had one vote, and they elected a leader together. But in 1972, the government wanted to flood the village to make a reservoir, so sadly they had to leave their community. Now, during the summer when the water levels are low, the village emerges from the water. Tourists come to see the old town and even visit an underwater museum. It's a sorry reminder for those who lost their homes, but at the same time an incredible sight to see.

185

Now let's go to China, to a special fishing village called Houtouwan. This village used to be a busy place with lots of fishermen and their families. But over time, people started leaving, and nature took over. The village was covered in plants! It's like a real-life jungle now. Only adventurous tourists visit this place to explore. It's like a museum, with old furniture and belongings, but nature's the owner now.

Next up is a place called Chernobyl in Ukraine. In 1986, there was a terrible nuclear disaster, and people had to leave their homes. The whole area got abandoned, but now wildlife has taken over the empty streets. Bears, lynxes, wolves, and more than 200 bird species live there now.

SHOPPING NIGHTMARE

In the early 1980s, a shiny new shopping centre called New World Mall opened in Bangkok, Thailand. But it didn't last very long! After just 15 years, it closed down forever. Why? Well, it had a lot of bad luck. There were fires and collapses, and the people kept building extra floors without permission. And to make things worse, those extra floors made the mall taller than the famous Grand Palace nearby! The neighbours got mad because it's not cool to be taller than a historical landmark.

But here's where it gets complicated. When they tore down some of the extra floors, the mall didn't have a roof anymore. Can you imagine a mall without a roof? The ground floor got completely flooded, like a huge swimming pool!

And you know what happens when there's stagnant water? Mosquitoes start throwing a party! The people who lived nearby didn't want those pesky bugs, so they came up with a brilliant idea. They started throwing fish into the flooded mall. Yep, fish! The fish loved their new home and started multiplying like crazy. There were so many koi fish, striped catfish, and other cool fish swimming around. It turned into a fishy wonderland!

MOST REMOTE PLACES
...in the world 🌍

Amundsen-Scott South Pole Station in Antarctica is a research station where scientists study the coldest place on Earth. The days and nights there last for six months each. Imagine not seeing the sun that long!

Tristan Da Cunha, Atlantic Ocean, is the most remote inhabited place on Earth. It's a small volcanic island with only 241 people living there. They have their own rules and take care of the land together. You can only reach this island by a six-day boat ride from South Africa. What an epic adventure!

Supai Village in Arizona is known as the most remote community in the 48 contiguous states of the US. It's located in a canyon, and the only way to get there is by helicopter or hiking a long trail. The village is the capital of the Havasupai Indian Reservation and has about 450 residents. Can you imagine getting mail delivered by a mule? It's like living in a place untouched by modern roads!

The Pitcairn Islands in the Southern Pacific Ocean have a fascinating history. The people who live there are descendants of the famous mutineers from the HMAV Bounty ship. The population is small, but they are trying to grow by giving away land for free. You can now visit this unique island by taking a cargo ship from New Zealand.

Devon Island in Canada is the largest uninhabited island on Earth. Scientists go there to conduct space experiments because it's the most Mars-like place we can access. They test all kinds of space tools and robots in the rugged and cold landscape.

Easter Island, or Rapa Nui, is a mysterious island with huge stone statues called moai. It's so far away from other land that it's known as the closest place to the oceanic pole of inaccessibility. You can imagine how remote and special it is to visit this UNESCO World Heritage site.

La Rinconada in the Peruvian Andes is no ordinary town – it's the highest permanent settlement in the whole world!

Can you imagine living at the base of a gigantic glacier that's more than five kilometres (three miles) above sea level? To reach La Rinconada, you have to embark on a thrilling four-hour drive on steep and dangerous mountain roads. Around 50,000 brave souls call La Rinconada home, even though they don't have running water or a sewage system. That's right, no pipes to bring water or take away waste!

It can get super chilly there, with the temperature hovering around 1°C (34°F)! degrees, but most places aren't heated. And they value electricity because it only arrived in 2002!

Now, here's the tricky part. La Rinconada has been described as a 'frozen wasteland' and an 'environmental catastrophe.' The streets become like rivers because there's no indoor plumbing, so sewage flows outside. And guess what? The garbage freezes and piles up along the roads because there's no municipal collection service. Yuck!

Why do people still choose to live there? There are gold mining opportunities! It's a tough job, but the allure of finding gold draws people to town, even with all the challenges.

The Kerguelen Islands in the Indian Ocean are so remote that they're called the Desolation Islands. Scientists live there to study the icy geography, including glaciers and tall peaks. You can only reach these islands by ship a few times a year.

Longyearbyen in Norway is the world's northernmost settlement. It's on an island called Spitsbergen, not too far from the North Pole. Despite the extreme cold and remoteness, people from 53 different countries call this place home. But there's an interesting rule – dying is forbidden there!

Yep, you heard it right. If someone gets really sick or is about to pass away, they are immediately flown by aeroplane or ship to another part of Norway.

Why is that? Well, it turns out that the extreme cold weather in Longyearbyen stops bodies from decomposing in the cemetery. It's so cold that even nature's way of recycling doesn't happen. Recently, scientists took tissue from a man who died a long time ago and found traces of a dangerous virus that caused an epidemic in 1917. So they decided it's best not to have bodies buried there anymore.

Now, here's another fun fact. In Longyearbyen, the citizens are allowed to move around with high-powered rifles. Whoa, that's some serious protection! Wanna know why? Well, over 3,000 polar bears are roaming around the area. So, just in case, they're ready to keep themselves safe.

Oh, and guess what? Cats are forbidden in Longyearbyen. Why? Well, those adorable furry friends pose a threat to the bird population. So, to protect the birds, cats aren't allowed. It's all about keeping the balance in nature.

Ittoqqortoormiit in Greenland is a tiny settlement surrounded by breathtaking landscapes. It's frozen for most of the year, and only 450 people live there. They have colourful houses and get to see amazing wildlife like polar bears and whales. They even have a local pub that opens once a week. To get there, you have to take a helicopter or a boat.

The Changtang in Tibet is called the 'Roof of the World' because it's so high up. The villages are at an average height of 4,700 metres. The climate there is extremely cold and the summers are short. It's home to nomads and amazing wildlife like snow leopards and yaks. The landscapes are beautiful, with giant lakes and highlands.

FAMILY OF CAPTAIN COOK

Palmerston Island is a tiny place in the Pacific Ocean made up of beautiful sandy islets connected by a coral reef. Since seaplanes can't land there, ships visit only a few times a year to bring supplies and visitors. Around 58 people live on the island, and they are all descendants of Captain James Cook. Isn't it cool to live on an island with such a fascinating history?

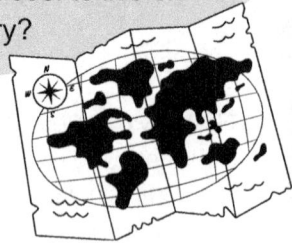

Villa Las Estrellas in Antarctica is a small village and research station. It's so remote that people have to have their appendix removed before arriving because the nearest hospital is 966 kilometres (600 miles) away, so there wouldn't be time to get to hospital in an appendix-related emergency!

It was established in 1984 and is home to less than 200 people. The town has 14 homes, a bank, a school, a post office, a gym, a hostel, and even a souvenir shop. Most of the people there are scientists or members of the Chilean military. But guess what? Dogs aren't allowed because they could harm the delicate wildlife. Instead, residents get to live alongside penguins and elephant seals!

190

INCREDIBLE ISLANDS

Borneo is the third-largest island on Earth, and it's as big as the state of Texas! It's divided among Malaysia, Indonesia, and the tiny sultanate of Brunei. You know what's cool? Borneo is home to more than 222 different kinds of mammals, and 44 of them can only be found there. And get this – there are about 6,000 plant species in Borneo, and many of them are unique to the island. It's a pretty amazing place.

Sumatra is an island in Indonesia that's even bigger than 473,000 square kilometres (182,000 square miles) – that's more than twice the size of Great Britain! It's home to more than 50 million people. In the jungles of Sumatra, you can find tigers, rhinos, elephants, and orangutans all living together. It's the only place on Earth where these amazing creatures share the same home. People are working hard to protect them because some of them, like the Sumatran tiger, are endangered.

Madagascar is a special island in the Indian Ocean. It's the fourth-largest island in the world, and it's like a biodiversity wonderland! Nearly 90% of the plants and 92% of the mammals in Madagascar are unique – they can't be found anywhere else. Some plants even grow only on mountaintops! But you know who steals the show? Lemurs! Madagascar is home to 104 different types of lemurs, and they're all found only on this incredible island.

Monuriki in Fiji became famous because it was the primary filming location for the movie 'Cast Away' with Tom Hanks. Can you imagine living on an island all alone for four years? In reality, there are other islands nearby, but Monuriki has become a popular tourist spot because of the movie magic.

New Zealand is a country made up of two main islands – North Island and South Island. Each island is bursting with unique species that you won't find anywhere else. All the native bats, reptiles, and amphibians in New Zealand can only be found there. And did you know that 88% of the freshwater fish are endemic? That means they're exclusive to New Zealand. Even the fungi in New Zealand are special – scientists haven't even classified most of them yet.

Tasmania is an island south of mainland Australia, and it's a treasure trove of biodiversity. You've probably heard of the Tasmanian devil – it's the largest carnivorous marsupial alive today, and it's famous for its fierce attitude. But Tasmania is also home to other unique creatures like the eastern quoll, platypus, and penguins. Oh, and get this – the Huon pine, a special tree, can live for a mind-boggling 3,000 years!

South Georgia Island! Who would've thought that the islands of Antarctica could have so much biodiversity? South Georgia Island is a remote place, and scientists have discovered a whopping 1,445 different species living in its coastal waters. From penguins and seals to fascinating creatures like seaworms and icefish, there's so much life here. South Georgia is a true wildlife paradise.

Coiba Island is located off the coast of Panama, and it's a haven for unique animals that have evolved with little human contact. The Coiba howler monkey is the most famous of these special creatures. What's cool about Coiba is that it used to be home to a prison, so very few people visited the island. That means the forests are still untouched, and more than 75% of the land is covered in pristine forests. And nearby, you can explore one of the largest coral reefs on the entire Pacific Coast – how awesome is that?

Navassa Island in the Caribbean. It's uninhabited and classified as a nature reserve. You need special permission to enter, and even the coastline has steep cliffs that make it hard for boats to land. Plus, it's a territorial dispute between the US and Haiti. Quite an intriguing place!

Ni'ihau is the westernmost Hawaiian island. It's super special because it's completely privately owned. Only about 130 people live there, and they speak Hawaiian as their native language. What a privilege to own this little paradise!

The Galápagos Islands in Ecuador are famous because they inspired Charles Darwin's theory of evolution. You can find amazing animals there, like the Galápagos land iguana, Galápagos tortoise, flightless cormorant, and unique finches known as 'Darwin's finches.' There's even a penguin species in the Northern Hemisphere, and they call the Galápagos Islands their home. These islands are a living laboratory of evolution!

Bouvet Island in the South Atlantic Ocean is covered in ice and almost untouched by humans. It's a nature preserve, and Norway takes care of it. Bouvet is so remote that the nearest land, Queen Maud Land in Antarctica, is over 1,600 kilometres (1,000 miles) away. You have to be pretty determined to travel somewhere so remote and chilly.

MOST UNUSUAL TOWNS

The Villages, Florida, US, is a town made especially for retired people who want to have a great time! It's so big that it's even larger than Manhattan Island in New York. The people there love their golf carts. They even made a world record for having the longest golf cart parade ever – a whopping 3,321 golf carts all lined up and cruising together. Now, here's a strange fact: in this unique town, kids are not allowed to live there. It's a place where only grown-ups go to relax and enjoy their retirement.

Ordos has been called the largest ghost town in all of China. Spooky! Okay, here's the deal. This city was built to fit over a million people. But shockingly only a teeny-tiny 2% of it was ever occupied. The rest just sits there, all lonely and abandoned. Even the completed buildings aren't fully occupied because they're too expensive.

But hey, the town isn't giving up. To attract people to come and live there, clever investors have reduced the prices. And get this, fresh graduates who want to start a business there even get free office space and internet connection. They're trying to make the town come alive again!

MONKEY MAYHEM

Marloth Park is a town right next to the famous Kruger National Park in South Africa, where all kinds of amazing animals like lions, hippos, and crocodiles roam freely. Exciting, isn't it? But here's the really strange part: in Marloth Park, the residents are not allowed to build fences around their houses. Even though there are these big, powerful animals around. The only thing separating the townspeople from the park is a small metre-high fence, just to keep humans out. It's like living side by side with nature!

In Marloth Park, it's totally normal to see wild animals strolling through the town. You might look out your window and see a giraffe or an elephant passing by! But be careful with your snacks because cheeky baboons are known to sneak into houses through windows to steal food from refrigerators.

IDENTICAL TWIN TOWNS...

There's a real Hallstatt in Austria, a UNESCO World Heritage Site.
But guess what? There's also a mock-up version in China, which was built to look just like the real Hallstatt, with its roads, church tower, and cute wooden houses. Can you imagine having a town that's like a copycat version of a famous place?

The Chinese Hallstatt cost a huge $940 million US dollars and surprised the people in the real Hallstatt, who didn't know their town was being copied. They were proud but wished the Chinese had asked first!

Let's head to a super unique town called Busingen am Hochrhein. It's a town that's in Germany but surrounded by Switzerland, like an island on land. It's connected to the rest of Germany by a teeny-tiny strip of land. It's only about 700 metres wide at its narrowest point, a distance most people could walk in 10 minutes. What's extra cool is that the residents enjoy public services from both Switzerland and Germany.

Monowi in Nebraska is a super tiny town, I'm talking really, really small. In fact, it's the tiniest place in the whole US! Monowi has only one resident. Yup, you heard it right! Her name is Elsie Eller, and she's 77 years young. Elsie does it all in Monowi. She runs the town's tavern, but that's not all – she also takes care of the town's library. It's filled with about 5,000 books that belonged to her late husband, Rudy. It's like a treasure trove of stories!

But wait, there's more! Elsie is not just a tavern owner and librarian. She's also the mayor, clerk, treasurer, and runs the council. Phew! That's a lot of hats to wear, isn't it? Back in the 1930s, Monowi had around 150 people living there. But by the year 2000, it had dwindled to just two: Elsie and her husband, Rudy. Sadly, Rudy passed away in 2004, leaving Elsie as the only resident in town. She's like the queen of Monowi, ruling over her little kingdom.

In Whittier in Alaska, US, almost all of the 200-plus people live in a gigantic 14-storey building called Begich Towers. Back in 1956, the building was an army barracks. But today, it's a whole town by itself!

Inside this tower, you'll find a police station, post office, grocery store, church, video rental shop, health centre, and a playground. Everything you need, all in one big building! To get there you can hop on a boat and sail through the sea. Or, you can go through a special tunnel that's about four kilometres long. But here's the catch: the tunnel has gates that open only twice every hour. That means you have to time it just right!

DEAD OR ALIVE?!

I've got a spine-chilling tale for you about a town called Colma in California, US. Brace yourself because this place has more... wait for it... dead people than living ones!

Way back during the exciting Gold Rush of 1849, tons of people flocked to San Francisco in search of shiny gold. But, sadly, along with the gold rush came diseases that brought a lot of sorrow and, well, death.

By the 1880s, the town of Colma had around 26 cemeteries, and they were almost full to the brim. That's a lot of resting places, my friend.

The big Californian city of San Francisco decided that they didn't want any more burials within their limits. They thought the land was too valuable for cemeteries. So, in March 1900, they made a rule saying, 'No more graves in the city!' Then, in January 1914, the politicians told the cemetery owners that they had to remove all the bodies buried in San Francisco, and they moved all the bodies to Colma.

Nowadays, if you visit Colma, you'll see that over 73% of the town's land is dedicated to cemeteries. It's like a sprawling city of graveyards, and it's quite a sight to behold. It's a place where history rests in peace.

INTRIGUING VILLAGES

In Western Ukraine, there's a village called Velikaya Kopanya. It's called the 'Land of the Twins' because there are so many twin pairs there. For generations, twins have been popping up like crazy! Not just in humans, but even cows have twin calves at a high rate! How strange is that? Some think it's because of a special well in the village that gives them this twin-birthing power.

A VERY SLEEPY VILLAGE

In Kazakhstan, there are two villages called Kalachi and Krasnogorsk which had a peculiar problem. Imagine people suddenly falling asleep during the day, even while walking or working! And they'd stay asleep for days! Everyone in the villages was affected, from kids to grown-ups, even the pets! Some kids had wild dreams about winged horses and worms.

For a long time, nobody knew why it was happening. Some thought it was the fake alcohol, and others thought it was mass dreaming. But guess what? Scientists finally figured it out! There was too much pollution in the air and water from old mines nearby. Thankfully, the villagers have been relocated and can go back to sleeping only when they mean to!

ZZZ

In a village called Bengkala in Indonesia, something amazing happens! Can you believe that 42 out of 3,000 people there have been deaf since they were born? That's way more than usual, around five times higher than anywhere else in the world, because of a special gene!

But in this village, being deaf isn't a problem at all! Deafness is so common that everyone knows an ancient sign language called kato kolok. It's their secret code for communicating with each other. Even in school, deaf kids, also called 'kolok,' learn and play together with hearing kids. They have a truly special community where everyone is equal.

In the heart of Amsterdam, there's a special village called Hogewey. It's not like any other village you know! Here, people with dementia can live happily and feel like they're in a normal place. Instead of nursing homes that feel sad, Hogewey is like a little world of its own.

Healthcare workers play different roles, like working in the salon, grocery store, restaurant, and movie theatre. Family and friends can visit when they want, and guess what? It's cheaper than regular care facilities! What a way to make something positive out of a challenging situation.

In a place called Yangsi in China, there's a unique village known as the 'Dwarf Village.' A remarkable 40% of the people there are shorter than 120 centimetres (four feet)!

Normally, there's just a tiny chance of being a dwarf, like one in 20,000, but not in Yangsi. Scientists can't figure out why this happens, but there are some wild theories! One fun legend is about a man named Wang who ate a special turtle, and that's how the village got 'cursed' with dwarfs. But don't worry, the youngest generation doesn't seem to have this curse!

WONDERS OF THE WORLD

ANCIENT WONDER

The only one still standing is the Great Pyramid of Giza. This massive structure was built around 2560 BC as a fancy tomb for a pharaoh named Khufu. It held the record as the tallest man-made thing for about 4,000 years. The pyramid is gigantic, with sides longer than two football fields, and it's made up of a whopping 2.3 million stone blocks.

MODERN WONDERS

Channel Tunnel: Imagine an underwater tunnel that connects the UK to France beneath the English Channel. It's like a secret passage for trains! There are two big tunnels for trains and a smaller one for services. This tunnel stretches for about 50 kilometres (31 miles), and a big chunk of it is underwater. What an amazing feat of engineering!

CN Tower: In Toronto, Canada, there's a tower that's like a giant antenna. It was built in 1976 and stands super tall at 553.3 metres (1815.3 feet). That's even taller than two football fields in a row! This tower sends out TV, radio, and wireless signals all across Toronto.

Empire State Building: Imagine a building with 102 storeys, almost like a towering bookshelf! The Empire State Building in New York City used to be the tallest in the world at 380 metres (1,250 feet). That's as tall as 75 giraffes stacked on top of each other! It's a symbol of the city and human achievement.

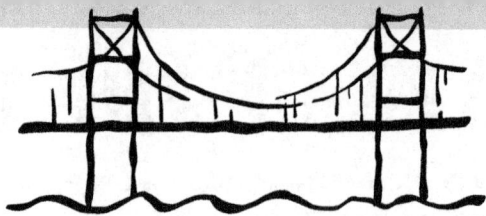

Golden Gate Bridge: The Golden Gate Bridge in San Francisco is like a giant rainbow stretching across the bay. It's 2.7 kilometres (1.7 miles) long and carries about 41 million cars every year. Before this bridge, people had to take ferries to cross the bay.

Itaipu Dam: Picture a massive dam that's as big as a mountain. The Itaipu Dam is located between Brazil and Paraguay and was finished in 1984. It's the biggest hydroelectric power plant in the world, creating even more electricity than China's Three Gorges Dam! This electricity helps both countries, giving Paraguay most of its power.

Netherlands North Sea Protection: The Netherlands is a network of land with waterways known as flowing between. Lots of the land is below sea level so the Dutch people built big dikes (barriers) to keep the sea away. One of them, called the Afsluitdijk, is like a super long wall that turned a sea into a giant lake! This made new places to live, which would have been underwater before!

Panama Canal: Imagine a shortcut for big ships that connect the Atlantic and Pacific Oceans. The Panama Canal is like a waterway magic trick! It was built from 1904 to 1914 and now belongs to Panama. It saves ships about 12,875 kilometres (8,000 miles) of travel around South America's tip. Ships go through special locks, and the whole journey takes about 15 hours.

INSPIRING PEOPLE

In this chapter, meet remarkable individuals who have turned barren landscapes into lush forests by planting thousands of trees, and discover incredible stories of women, men, and even children whose extraordinary deeds will fill you with awe and motivation.

SELFLESS ACTS

A rich person from Sweden named Johan Eliasch did something amazing. He created a charity, and through it, bought a huge part of the Amazon Rainforest to protect it from being cut down so that it can keep growing and thriving for many years to come. This has saved the creatures living there, as well as the trees and other plants that help keep our planet healthy and balanced.

SPECIAL SERVICE

In Japan, a train station was going to close, but they kept it open for a special reason. There was a girl who used that train station to go to school. They wanted to help her, so they kept the station running until she finished school. Now that's outstanding customer service!

The people who make cars, Volvo, made a special seat belt that helps keep people safe in cars. But guess what? They didn't keep it just for themselves. They shared their idea with everyone, so all cars could be safer, even if Volvo didn't make more money from it.

A carpenter named Dale Schroeder used all his savings to help 33 students go to college. Those students, known as 'Dale's kids,' grew up to become doctors, teachers, and other great things. Dale's kindness changed their lives.

DID YOU KNOW MORGAN FREEMAN CARES ABOUT BEES?

He transformed his big piece of land into a safe place for bees. He planted special plants and even became a beekeeper with 26 beehives to help the bees live happily. Bees pollinate a big percentage of the plants that feed us. Sadly the bee population is declining because of human interference in nature, so acts like Morgan's are incredibly important.

When the famous Notre Dame cathedral in Paris was damaged in a fire, in 2019, a video game company named Ubisoft stepped in to help. They used their knowledge and plans of the building to help fix it and even gave money to make the repairs happen.

Costa Rica decided to use clean and green energy for almost all their electricity. They're role models, showing the world that we can power our countries with sources that are renewable and don't cause huge amounts of pollution. The efforts are clear. In 2015, the country ran entirely on renewable energy for 299 days, using sources like hydroelectric, wind, geothermal, and solar power.

Can you believe that someone could live to be 100 and still work on important things? Dr. Jacinto Convit did just that! He made heaps of scientific progress on a vaccine against a serious sickness called leishmaniasis. And he didn't stop there. He kept working even when he turned 100!

A young person named William Kamkwamba from a village in Malawi, Africa, didn't have much money or go to a fancy school, but he taught himself from books. He used his skills to build windmills and bring electricity to his village. His story inspired many others!

Gabe Sonnier worked as a janitor in a school in the US. But guess what? He got inspired by the school's principal and decided to become a teacher himself. He studied while cleaning and later became the principal of that same school. What a career change!

Harris Rosen changed a neighbourhood in Florida, US for the better. By funding free childcare and free college spots for graduates, he reduced the crime levels and increased the high school graduation rate to an astonishing 100%!

Way back in 1665, a bad sickness called the Black Death came to a village called Eyam in England. Instead of letting it spread to other villages, the people of Eyam did something amazing. They stayed in their village to keep the sickness from spreading. Even though it was really hard and they risked their lives, they protected others by staying put.

A kind friar named Maximilian Kolbe was taken prisoner during the Second World War. When ten of his fellow prisoners were chosen to be starved to death, he volunteered to take the place of a man with a family. He gave up his own life to save someone else's. He's remembered for his kindness and is even considered a saint.

A homeless man named Elmer Alvarez, returned a lost $10,000 US dollars cheque to its owner, Roberta Hoskie. Touched by his honesty, she provided him with housing and a job and later made him a director of her affordable housing foundation in Connecticut, US.

A man in Australia who got stuck between a train and the platform. It sounds really scary, right? But guess what happened? The people waiting for the train didn't panic. They all worked together and found the collective strength to push the train just enough to free the man's leg. They saved the day and kept him safe!

TRUE ANGEL

There's a man named Mohamed Bzeek in Los Angeles, US who has a special mission. He takes care of kids who are very ill and might not have much time left. He's like a guardian angel, making sure these children feel loved and cared for, no matter who they are. He's looked after more than 40 children, and a special movie called 'Guardian of Angels' shares his story.

THEY'RE NOT PEOPLE, BUT THEY NEED A MENTION ...

There was a famous dolphin named Pelorus Jack in New Zealand. He helped ships find their way through dangerous waters for 24 years! Sailors waited for him to show up and guide them. He even got special protection because he was so important.

Two young gorillas did something incredible. The pair lived in the mountain forest in Rwanda, Africa. After one of their gorilla friends got caught by a poacher's trap, these smart gorillas learned how to take the traps apart. Even though they were only four years old, they protected their forest by stopping those dangerous traps.

FOREST FATHERS

Once upon a time in Java, Indonesia, there was a man named Sadiman who did something amazing. People thought he was crazy at first, but he had a big dream – to plant a whole forest all by himself! The land he started with was dry and lifeless, with no water and caused lots of problems for the nearby community. Starting in the late 1990s, Sadiman worked hard for over two decades, planting over 11,000 trees. He chose special trees like banyan and ficus that could store water and bring life back to the land. People laughed and didn't believe in him, but he didn't give up. He knew that his forest could make a real difference.

Guess what? Sadiman's efforts paid off! Underground springs started flowing, bringing water to the villagers for drinking and farming. Now they could grow crops more often and have enough to eat. Everyone realised how Sadiman's work improved their lives. Sadiman didn't stop there. He taught many others to protect forests, showing us that even one person can make a huge impact and create a greener and happier environment for all!

205

An Indian man named Jadav Molai Payeng, the Forest Man, had a very similar idea. He had a mission – to turn a big piece of barren land into a beautiful forest! Every day, since way back in 1979, he planted a tiny tree sapling. Can you believe it? That's planting a tree every single day for more than 40 years! He worked tirelessly and transformed a huge area, about the size of 15 football fields, into a lush, green forest, attracting all kinds of amazing animals. There were birds, butterflies, monkeys, and even elephants!

But Jadav didn't keep his forest-making knowledge a secret. He wanted everyone, especially children, to learn the importance of planting trees and taking care of nature. He believed that by honouring and protecting nature, we can survive and thrive. He has spread this wisdom worldwide, helping to create forests in many corners of our planet.

How many trees can you plant in a day? In La Crete, Canada, there lived a record-breaking tree planter named Antoine Moses. He had a big dream – to plant as many trees as possible in just 24 hours! And guess what? He did it! Antoine planted a whopping 23,060 trees solo.

WHY PLANT TREES?

Did you know that trees are our best allies when it comes to fighting climate change? They can absorb a whole bunch of carbon dioxide, which is a bad gas that makes our planet too warm. Cool, right?

Here's a fun fact: a mature tree can gobble up about 22 kilograms (49 pounds) of carbon dioxide every year. That's like a big, green vacuum cleaner for the air! But guess what? Our Earth produces a whopping 36 billion tonnes (39.7 billion imperial tons) of carbon dioxide each year. That's a huge number!

To make a dent in all that carbon dioxide, we would need around 1.6 trillion trees. Woah, that's a lot of trees! But remember, this calculation assumes humans don't start to emit more than we already do, and it doesn't count other problematic gases or the fact that trees need time to grow big and strong.

Now, let's think about the people. There are about 7.9 billion of us on this planet. If we could magically divide all those trees evenly among everyone, each person would need to plant around 202 trees. That's like having your own little forest!

That would mean planting about 29 trees per year if you lived for at least 70 more years. Just one tree per month! Sounds possible, right? We have to remember to think about things like available land and resources, and using the right species of tree for each environment. So, while it's a cool idea, we need to be realistic too. But trees are an important part of the solution and every smartly planted tree is worth celebrating!

WOMEN OF WONDER

Fatima al-Fihri lived back in the ninth century in Morocco. She could have lived a fancy life because she had lots of money from her dad. But instead, she did something great. She used her money to build a special place for people to learn. It started as a mosque and a learning centre, and eventually, it became the world's very first university! It's still open today, and people from all over the world come to study there. Even though it's been over a thousand years, people still remember her with special awards and scholarships.

Maya Angelou was a super-talented lady from Missouri, US. She did a whole bunch of things like writing, dancing, and even being a civil rights activist, fighting for African–American equality. You might know her for her book called 'I Know Why the Caged Bird Sings.' She had to deal with racism throughout her life, but she didn't let that stop her from trying to change things. She wrote lots of books, made a movie, and even read a poem at a big event for a president. In 2010, another president gave her a special medal.

Emmeline Pankhurst was like a fierce warrior for women's rights! She fought with all her strength to make sure women could vote, just like men. But she didn't just talk the talk; she walked the walk. She organised protests, went on hunger strikes, and did whatever it took to get people to notice and make a difference. Her hard work paid off. In 1918, thanks to her and other strong women, some women in the UK finally got the right to vote. Emmeline's spirit and determination blazed a trail for equality.

Amelia Earhart was a brave American lady who became a famous pilot. She played basketball and went to college, which was a difficult thing for women in the early twentieth century. She broke lots of records in flying and inspired many other women to try jobs that only men used to do.

Jane Austen wrote stories in England 200 years ago, at a time when it was unusual for women to be authors. She didn't write many books because she passed away when she was still pretty young, but her books have been famous for generations. She had a way of telling tales that lots of other people started to copy. People loved her stories back then, and they still do today. Her books even turned into movies and plays!

Rachel Carson was a US writer who cared a lot about nature. She wrote a book called 'Silent Spring' in 1962 that made a big splash. In her book, she explained how some things people used to kill bugs were actually hurting animals and people too. Even though some big companies didn't like what she said, she didn't give up. Her book is still very important today, even after 60 years!

Rosalind Franklin was a smart scientist from England. She helped discover the shape of something called DNA, which is like a building plan for living things. Some other scientists got famous for this discovery, even though she did a lot of the work. She got sick and passed away, but her work continues to be important in science today.

Helen Keller couldn't see or hear, but that didn't stop her. She learned to read with her fingers and talk with her hands. Then she went to a special US college just for women. More amazingly – she fought for the rights of all people. She was an author too, so you can read all about her!

Jane Goodall was just 26 years old when she left England for Africa to study chimpanzees. She wasn't even a scientist, but she noticed some curious things about how chimps use tools and are super smart. Her research has been going on for over 60 years! Her discoveries changed the way we think about animals. Nowadays, even at 89 years old, she travels around the world to make sure animals are treated well and continues to spread her message to the world.

Sojourner Truth was born into slavery in the US, but that didn't hold her back. She managed to break free and dedicated her life to fighting against slavery and for the rights of women. Even though she couldn't read or write, she shared her incredible story and met some really important people who also wanted to make the world fairer. Her passionate speeches about fairness and kindness inspired many others to stand up for what's right, turning her into a true hero for change.

Rosa Parks was like a spark that started a fire for change. In 1955, when she decided not to move from her bus seat because of racist laws, she became a symbol of courage. But her bravery didn't stop there. Rosa worked really hard for civil rights, like making sure people were treated fairly no matter their skin colour. She joined forces with other heroes like Martin Luther King Jr. in the fight for equality in the US. Her actions and her strong voice made a huge difference, and they even led to changes in the law. She didn't just make things better for herself; she made things better for everyone.

Wangari Maathai planted a ton of trees in Kenya. She was the first woman in East and Central Africa to reach the highest level of education called a Ph.D. She started a group to help women plant trees and fight problems like poverty and the destruction of nature. Even though some people tried to stop her, she carried on and won a Nobel prize for her hard work.

Florence Nightingale was way more than just a nurse. When she went into British hospitals during the war, she didn't just take care of sick people. She made the hospitals cleaner and safer for everyone. After the war, she kept on working hard to make nursing better for everyone. She believed that everyone should have good healthcare, and she made it her mission to make that happen. She taught other nurses and made sure patients were treated well.

Maryam Mirzakhani was a maths star from Iran. She loved maths and was so good at it that she won gold medals in maths contests around the world. She went to school in Iran and the US and became a professor at Stanford University, which is a big deal. In 2014, she won this super important award called the Fields Medal, which is like the Nobel Prize for mathematicians. What a whiz!

$$x = \frac{-b \pm \sqrt{b^2 - 4ac}}{2a}$$

Chien-Shiung Wu was a Chinese-American physicist who people called the 'First Lady of Physics.' She did a lot of incredible work but folks didn't always give her enough credit just because she was a woman. For example, in 1957, some guys she worked with won the Nobel Prize, and she helped them do it! Fortunately, she has since been recognized for her immense contribution to physics.

Grace Hopper was a computer whiz and a big deal in the US Navy. She's the reason we call computer problems 'bugs.' One time, a real moth caused a computer to mess up, and she called it a bug. She helped make the world's first computer that businesses could use, which was a huge deal. She also did really important things with computer languages, like COBOL. She helped make computers what they are today, and that's pretty awesome!

Beulah Louise Henry was born not long after Thomas Edison invented the light bulb. But Beulah was a real inventor too, and people even called her 'Lady Edison.' She came up with all sorts of clever things like a machine to make ice cream, a sponge that had soap inside it, and a sewing machine that didn't need a bobbin. She got 49 patents for her original inventions, and she had even more ideas that she didn't patent, so she was really, really creative.

Marie Curie was a scientist from Poland, and she was brilliant at her job. She discovered some amazing things about tiny particles called atoms. She was so good that she won not just one, but two Nobel Prizes. She was the first woman ever to get one of those prizes, and she even got them in two different fields of science.

FEARLESS FRIDA

Frida Kahlo was an artist from Mexico who painted lots of pictures of herself. She had a unique style and was proud of who she was. She painted herself with a unibrow and moustache, which was unusual but she was cool for not caring what others thought. She also wore colourful dresses that showed off her Mexican culture. Her paintings are famous all over the world, and she's a symbol of art and women's rights.

Susan LaFlesche Picotte was just eight years old when she saw something really unfair happen. In the early 1870s, a Native American woman couldn't get medical help just because of who she was. Susan decided she wanted to change that. She became the very first Native American woman to become a doctor. She went back to her community and worked super hard to help sick people and make healthcare better for Native Americans. Her dedication made a big difference, and she was a heroine for her people.

212

Harriet Tubman escaped slavery and, even more incredibly, helped many others escape too! She even worked as a spy and led a daring mission during the US Civil War. Later on, she fought for women's right to vote. Harriet's bravery and determination didn't stop with her own freedom; she dedicated her life to helping others find their way to freedom as well.

Peggy Whitson changed space exploration. For a long time, it was mostly a boys' club, and it wasn't fair. But then along came Peggy. She's been on the International Space Station and stepped out into space not just once, but ten times! This has earned her the Guinness World Record for Most Spacewalks by a Female Astronaut. She's a real space trailblazer, showing us what girls can do in the stars.

MARVELLOUS MEN

Mahatma Gandhi was an Indian politician who played a huge role in India's fight for independence from British rule. He led a movement that eventually succeeded in 1947, giving India its freedom. Gandhi's peaceful approach to change, known as nonviolent resistance, showed how powerful and effective peaceful methods could be.

Sir Isaac Newton is someone you've probably heard of. The British scientist who lived way back in the seventeenth and eighteenth centuries. He made a huge impact on history with his amazing ideas. Newton was a real genius who did important work in maths, physics, astronomy, and even theology. He made groundbreaking discoveries that still affect the way we understand the world today. One of his most famous contributions was figuring out how gravity works. He also calculated the speed of sound and did some incredible studies on light.

Martin Luther King Jr. is a really important person from the twentieth century. He did something huge by leading a movement for equal rights. He got a whole generation of people thinking about fairness and equality, especially when it came to different races. King was born in Atlanta, US, in 1929 and grew up at a time when laws separated people based on their skin colour. His movement helped end those unfair laws, and he even won the Nobel Peace Prize.

You've probably heard of Shakespeare – he's like the king of writing! His words help us understand ourselves and our society better. He wrote things over 400 years ago that still make us think today. He came up with lots of phrases we use every day, like 'catch a cold' or 'break the ice.' So, his legacy lives on through the way we talk.

Nikola Tesla was a Serbian–American in the nineteenth and twentieth centuries. He made some incredible contributions to electromagnetism research. Tesla's inventions ranged from electricity to radio transmission, showing his innovative mind. What our lives be like today without him?

Francis Bacon was a remarkable figure from England. He wasn't just a philosopher – he was also a political leader and a scientist. Bacon is known as the 'father of empiricism' because he helped promote the scientific method in the late sixteenth century. His work laid the foundation for how we investigate and understand the world around us.

The fourteenth Dalai Lama, named Tenzin Gyatso, is the spiritual leader of Tibetan Buddhism. He's known for promoting peaceful protests and standing up for important causes. He even won the Nobel Peace Prize for peacefully opposing a tough situation in Tibet. He's not just about religion – he talks passionately about things like women's rights, the environment, and more important topics.

Mozart stands out when you think about famous classical composers, right? People consider him one of the greatest ever. He was super talented, starting to make music when he was only five years old! By the time he passed away at 35, he had made more than 600 pieces of music. Many of his compositions are still really popular. Other famous composers like Beethoven and Chopin were inspired by his work.

Louis Pasteur was a French biologist in the nineteenth century who made significant contributions to medical science. He's famous for developing cures for diseases like rabies and anthrax, which saved countless lives. Pasteur's work paved the way for our understanding of infectious diseases and how to fight against them.

Edward Jenner was a pioneer who made a huge difference in medicine. He created the first vaccine for smallpox in 1796, which was a big step towards protecting people from this deadly disease. But his achievement didn't stop there – Jenner's breakthrough also opened the door for the development of many other vaccines that we benefit from today.

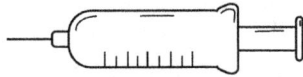

Sigmund Freud was an Austrian physician who is most known for his pioneering psychoanalysis in the early twentieth century. This is a way of understanding our thoughts and behaviours by exploring our subconscious mind. Freud delved deep into the study of dreams, helping us unravel the mysteries of our inner thoughts.

Leonardo Da Vinci was a true Renaissance man from Italy, born in 1452. He was not only a painter but also a scientist, inventor, and an all-around genius. Da Vinci's name is often mentioned when talking about incredible art, with masterpieces like the Mona Lisa and the Last Supper being some of his most famous works.

Socrates was a philosopher in ancient Greece born in 470 BC, who became famous for his unique way of thinking called the Socratic method. Instead of just accepting ideas, he questioned everything to help people think deeply. What's even more fascinating is that Socrates calmly accepted his own, showing his commitment to his beliefs.

Neil Armstrong was a US pilot and astronaut who made history by becoming the first person to walk on the moon. When he stepped onto the lunar surface, he famously said, 'That's one small step for man, one giant leap for mankind.' His achievement showed how far human exploration could go.

Rumi was born in Persia (now Iran) in the thirteenth century and was a spiritual man who followed the Sufi religion. His poetry captured people's hearts. He's still one of the most beloved poets of modern times, showing how poetry can touch our souls and help us understand deeper feelings.

Confucius was a wise person from ancient China whose ideas were so powerful that his followers created a book of them called The Analects. These thoughts became really important in China and beyond. He shaped how people thought about life, ethics, and how to live in a good way.

Galileo, born in the sixteenth century, was an Italian scientist who changed the way we see the world. He helped show that the Earth isn't at the centre of everything. Galileo also worked on the science of motion and materials, bringing new insights to these fields.

EVOLUTION OF IDEAS

Charles Darwin went on an epic trip. On his travels, he came up with an idea that explains how animals and plants change over time to become different species in a process called evolution. Back when Darwin shared this idea, many people saw it as a battle between religion and science and thought that we couldn't live in a world with both... the idea caused a lot of arguments. But he bravely shared his evidence with the world anyway. Evolution is a big part of modern biology.

$E=m.c^2$

Albert Einstein was an incredibly smart German scientist who did some mind-blowing stuff. He came up with the theory of relativity, a super cool idea still important today. His famous equation $E=mc^2$ earned him a Nobel Prize in 1921. He wrote over 300 papers about science. He also cared about people, spoke up for human rights, and wanted a peaceful world, opposing atomic bombs. So, he was a super-smart scientist and a good person who wanted a better world for all.

Nelson Mandela is another incredible person who fought for equal rights. He made a huge impact by standing up against a system of racial separation in South Africa. His actions caused big changes. He was put in prison for a long time, but even there, he didn't give up. He educated himself, went on strikes, met with other leaders, and did everything he could to fight against that unfair system. Eventually, he became South Africa's first black President after he was released from prison.

COURAGEOUS CHILDREN

Sisters Melati and Isabel Wijsen knew about the big problem of plastic in the seas when they were just 10 and 12 years old. In 2013, they started a group called 'Bye Bye Plastic' to fight against it. They pick up plastic and tell people not to use so much. They've talked about this at schools, meetings, and even in politics. What they started in Bali, Indonesia is now a worldwide campaign to stop plastic pollution.

SUPER MARKET

Emma Gonzales became an important American activist for gun control after a sad shooting at a school in 2018. Her strong words made a lot of people think about making changes to keep schools safe.

Samantha Smith was a young American girl from Maine. In 1982, she wrote a letter to the leader of the Soviet Union asking why the US and the Soviet Union weren't getting along. Her letter became famous when it was printed in a big newspaper in the Soviet Union, and the leader there wrote back! She even got to visit the Soviet Union, which was a big deal. She showed that people from different places could be friends.

Sophie Scholl was a brave girl in Germany during the Second World War. She and her friends created a peaceful group called White Rose. They wrote leaflets to stand up against a bad government, even though it was really dangerous. She believed in what she was doing and thought it would inspire others to make a difference. She was killed by her government during the war, but her bravery has influenced many others to speak out for what's right.

Emma Watson is a famous British actress known for her role as Hermione Granger in the Harry Potter movies. As well as acting, she has been campaigning for women's rights since she was a teenager. She helps the United Nations and speaks out about fairness for women, even starting a campaign to get everyone involved.

Nkosi Johnson (born Xolani Nkosi) was born with a sickness called HIV/AIDS in 1989, which he got from his parents. When he was 6, a school didn't let him in because they were afraid of his sickness. So, he talked about treating people with HIV fairly. With his foster mother, he made a place where mothers and kids with HIV could be safe. Even though he passed away young, he won a prize for children who work for peace, and Nelson Mandela said he was a big inspiration.

Ruby Bridges is a brave American civil rights activist. In 1960, she became the first black child to go to a school that used to be only for white kids in Louisiana. Even though people were mean to her, she helped change the rules about how schools could be for everyone, no matter their skin colour.

Iqbal Masih was born in 1983 and had a very tough childhood as a child labourer in Pakistan. He got away from that bad situation and became a strong fighter against child labour and for kids' right to go to school. He led a group that helped thousands of children and worked to end child labour all around the world.

Joan of Arc, born in 1412, was an amazing young woman who did something extraordinary at just 16 years old. She met with the French Dauphin, the heir to the French throne. Joan's belief and determination inspired him to fight against the English, which eventually led to a victory at Orleans, just as she had said it would. Sadly, she was executed at only 19, but her dream of freeing France came true and had a big impact.

Hector Pieterson was a young black South African who tragically died when he was just 13 years old during a protest in 1972. This protest was a strong way of saying no to the unfair treatment of black people in South Africa. A picture of him being carried away became a powerful symbol of fairness and equality.

Om Prakash Gurjar was born in India and had to work as a slave, just like his family. But he didn't give up. He joined others to help kids who were stuck in the same situation and fought for kids' rights. He got the 2006 International Children's Peace Prize for his incredible work.

Saint Thérèse of Lisieux is also known as 'The Little Flower'. Born in 1873, at the young age of 15 she asked the Pope for special permission to join a convent early. She passed away at 23, but her writings about her spiritual journey became very popular because of her simple yet deep ideas.

Greta Thunberg is a teenager from Sweden who cares a lot about the planet. She started skipping school in 2018 to protest against climate change. She got a lot of people to join her, and they even had a huge march. She continues her work to raise awareness about protecting the environment and has become a global ambassador, inspiring millions to take action for a sustainable future.

Anne Frank was a Jewish girl who wrote about her life during a really tough time. She had to hide from some very mean people called the Gestapo when the Nazis took over the Netherlands. She didn't make it through the Second World War, and she passed away in a place called Bergen-Belsen. But her dad decided to share her diaries with the world, and that let everyone know just how hard it was for young Jewish people during the Holocaust, and her diaries became super popular all over the world.

Malala Yousafzai was a brave girl who wanted girls in Pakistan to have a chance to go to school. She spoke out even when it was really dangerous, and in 2012 she got shot for it. But you know what? She didn't give up. She continued to fight for what she believed in. She even won the Nobel Peace Prize for being so brave, and she started a group to help girls everywhere get the education they deserve. What courage!

INSPIRING WORLD RECORDS

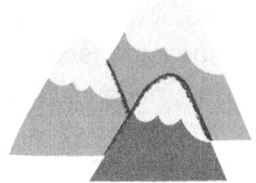

Most Mount Everest Climbs: Often the ultimate goal for mountaineers... Kami Rita Sherpa and Lhakpa Sherpa hold records for conquering Everest multiple times. Lhakpa Sherpa, a woman, has reached the summit nine times, while Kami Rita Sherpa has done it a staggering 24 times!

Longest Wheelchair Ramp Jump: Aaron Fotheringham was born with spina bifida but he didn't let that stop him. He started performing daring wheelchair stunts. In 2018, he astounded us by jumping 21 metres (70 feet) off a ramp. His resilience and determination are truly heroic.

Longest Career as a TV Broadcaster: David Attenborough's broadcasting career has spanned an incredible length of time, starting in 1953 and continuing to the present day. His numerous nature documentaries, like 'Planet Earth,' have made him a beloved figure in UK television history. By showing nature in incredible detail he's inspired a generation of nature-lovers.

Most Fruits and Veggies Donated in a Day: This is a fantastic story: On September 7, 2016, in Sacramento, California, US, a group did something amazing. In just one day, they gave away a massive 224,064 kilograms of fruits and veggies (that's almost 494,000 pounds!). They shared all this healthy food with 220 partner agencies and local food banks to help folks who needed it.

Most FIFA Wins by a Single Player: Pelé, the Brazilian soccer legend, has won the most World Cups. His victories in 1958, 1962, and 1970 make him one of the few players with multiple championship wins. His soccer prowess is legendary.

Most Guinness Records by a Single Person: Ashrita Furman from Japan has earned nearly 1,000 Guinness records, showcasing his remarkable talents and determination. His diverse achievements, from climbing Mount Fuji on a pogo stick to underwater hula hooping, make him a true record-breaking champion. What a combo!

Fastest Land Speed Record: In 1997, fighter pilot Andy Green reached achieved extraordinary speed on land in Thrust SSC, a jet-powered car. He drove at almost 1,228 kilometres per hour (763 miles per hour). That's some need for speed!

Largest Humanitarian Effort Ever: After the First World War in Iraq, the United Nations World Food Programme (WFP) jumped into action. They started the largest and most expensive mission to help people ever! It all began on April 1, 2003, and wrapped up in late October of the same year. They delivered a whopping 2.2 million tonnes of food (2.4 billion imperial tons) and did it all for just $1.5 billion US dollars.

ACRO AT 80

Oldest Flying Trapeze Star: Meet Betty Goedhart from California, US. She has soared into the record books as the oldest female flying trapeze artist at 84 years and 249 days old. Her story shows us that age should never stop us from chasing our dreams. Since she was young, Betty believed that hard work and determination could make anything possible. That's why, at 78, she decided to take up trapeze classes and prove that age is just a number.

Most Northerly Climate Protest: Mya-Rose Craig, a bird scientist from England, took her passion for birds to all seven continents. In 2020, she protested climate change in the Arctic Ocean. That's how committed she is to saving bird habitats and our planet.

First Food Grown in Space: In 1975 the crew of Soviet space station Salyut 4 managed to grow a small crop of spring onions, which they ate for a crew member's birthday.

On October 10, 1995, the US Space Shuttle Columbia blasted off from Cape Canaveral, and it had a special cargo – five leaves from potato plants called Norland. These leaves got to grow in a unique space plant incubator called Astroculture. It was like a tiny garden in space, where scientists took care of things like water, nutrients, and light. During its 16-day trip around Earth, those leaves even started growing tiny potatoes. It was the very first time a root vegetable food crop successfully grew in the weightless space environment. How cool is that?

First Person to Break the Sound Barrier in Freefall: Felix Baumgartner dared to break the sound barrier (the speed of sound) during a freefall from 38.6 kilometres (24 miles) above Earth in 2012. His other achievements include smashing records for high-speed parachute jumps.

Oldest Pro DJ: Sumiko Iwamura, aged 83 and hailing from Tokyo, Japan, is no ordinary grandma. By day, she runs a restaurant and cooks up delicious dishes, but by night, she transforms into DJ Sumirock, a rock star on the turntables in a club. She finds so much energy in doing something fresh and different, even though becoming a DJ late in life wasn't something she planned. She encourages us all to try new things and never give up, reminding us that opportunities are waiting around every corner.

SOME BONUS RECORDS, JUST BECAUSE...

Tallest Dog Ever: Zeus, the 70-kilogram (155-pound) Great Dane, was a giant with a gentle personality. Standing at over 90 centimetres (three feet) tall on all fours, he was a sight to behold. His impressive height and quirks like drinking from the tap make us appreciate the uniqueness of our furry friends.

Longest Moustache: Ram Singh Chauhan of India boasts a truly epic 4-metre (14-foot) moustache, braided into 'beardlocks'. It's a remarkable display of personal style that sets him apart. The record for the longest non-braided moustache goes to Paul Slosar, US, with a moustache of 63.5 centimetres (25 inches).

Longest Nose: Mehmet Özyürek of Turkey holds the record for the largest nose, at 8.8 centimetres (3.5 inches) long. His confident attitude toward his unique feature reflects his positive outlook.

POWERFUL PROTESTS

Gathering together to say that something is not right is our oldest way of asking for change. When protests are peaceful, they are extra powerful. They are a symbol of the caring world we are trying to create. Sometimes it feels like a protest has failed, but often it has changed the hearts and minds of people and will help us build a better future.

George Floyd Protests (2020): People throughout the US got angry after a man named George Floyd was killed by a police officer. They went out in the streets to say, 'Hey, this isn't right!' and to talk about how some people are treated unfairly because of their skin colour. It made a lot of people think about how we can make our world less racist.

Prague Spring and Uprising (1968): People in Czechoslovakia protested to have more freedom from the Soviet Union. Even though the Soviets used tanks to stop them, they took to the streets. It showed how much people value their freedom from control!

Women's March on Washington, US (2017): Right after a new president was sworn in, a huge group of women and their friends gathered to say, 'Hey, we're important too!' They wanted to make sure everyone knows that women should be treated with respect and fairness. People from all over the world joined, and it became one of the biggest gatherings for change, ever!

Storming of the Bastille (1789): In France, there was a big fight against the king because people didn't like how he ruled. They took over a prison called the Bastille. It started a big revolution that created a fairer country.

Orange Revolution (2004): In Ukraine, there was a big argument about who should be the leader. People protested because they thought the election wasn't fair. It was a sea of orange clothes and flags. Their protests led to a new election and a new leader. It was a great victory for fairness!

Gandhi's Salt March (1930): Imagine walking hundreds of miles to the beach to get some salt. Gandhi did just that to show he didn't like how the British were making people pay a lot for salt. It got a lot of people thinking that maybe India should be in charge of itself.

Tiananmen Square (1989): In China, students wanted more say in how their country was run. They gathered in a big square and asked for change. But the government didn't like it and sent soldiers to stop them. The protesters were incredibly brave as they knew it was a risky move. The results were tragic as hundreds, possibly thousands, were killed.

Berlin Wall Protests (1989): During the Cold War, a wall was built to separate two parts of Berlin, but people wanted it gone. They protested, and eventually, the wall was opened up, bringing East and West Berlin back together. You can still see traces of the wall in Berlin today!

Iraq War Protests (2003): People all over the world said they didn't want a big war to happen in Iraq. They marched in the streets to show they wanted peace. Even though they couldn't stop the war, they wanted to show that they didn't agree with it and the suffering it caused. It is estimated that between 3 January and 12 April 2003, 36 million people across the globe took part in almost 3,000 protests. That's a lot of people speaking out!

Protestant Reformation (1517): A long time ago, a guy named Martin Luther didn't like some things the church was doing like being able to buy forgiveness for sins. So, he wrote down 95 things he thought should change. This eventually led to a big split in the Christian church to create the Catholic and Protestant branches that still exist to this day.

AND NOW FOR ANOTHER MARTIN LUTHER...

March on Washington (1963): More than 200,000 folks in the US came together to say, 'Hey, we should treat everyone the same!' Martin Luther King Jr. talked about fairness and freedom in a famous speech. This big march helped make new laws that gave rights to black people and it still inspires people to fight for equality today.

South Africa's National Day of Protest (1950): In South Africa, many people stayed home from work to show they didn't like a law that let the government sneakily investigate political groups. It was a big step in the fight against unfair rules.

Boston Tea Party (1773): A long time ago in the US, some folks were mad about a tea tax from England. So, they dressed up like Native Americans and threw a bunch of tea into the harbour to say, 'We don't want your tea or your taxes!' This was a big event in the lead-up to the American Revolution and American independence.

Athens Polytechnic Occupation (2008–2009): Young people and workers protested against government policies and the economic situation of their country by refusing to leave the university building. They wanted real change. Their protest showed a demand for something better. It made world media and their commitment brought lots of attention to their message.

Emily Wilding Davison, UK (1913): This brave woman gave up her life when she jumped in front of the king's horse. Her message was, 'Women should be able to vote!' Her actions started a movement for women's rights.

March for Science (2017): Lots of folks got together to celebrate science. They wanted to remind everyone that science is like our genius best friend that helps us understand things like climate change and staying healthy. People all over the world joined in, saying, 'Science is important, and we should listen to it!'

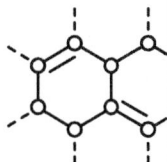

A BRIGHTER FUTURE

Whenever you watch the news, see the headlines or talk about the world, it may feel like we're in a lot of trouble. And it's true... we have work to do. But news stories don't focus on the bright side of life. Looking at the big picture of the last few centuries or decades, we can see that in many countries our lives have seriously improved.

SILVER LININGS

Ever heard the expression 'Every cloud has a silver lining'? This silver lining is a spark of hope when things seem bad, tricky or confusing. For most of these examples, we wish the situation were different. But when problems are so big that they're outside of your control, it's nice to see the good alongside the bad.

Languages Mix Up: In some places, there are rare languages only spoken by few people. It can be sad when these languages die out, as people feel like they are losing their identity. But, when some smaller languages disappear, people from different groups all learn the same language. This means they can work together better and get better jobs, bringing more income and a better quality of life to their communities.

Conflict Clears the Air: Believe it or not, during wars and fights, the air can sometimes get cleaner. This happens because people leave and stop doing things that make the air dirty.

The World Gets More Open-Minded: Even though the world can sometimes seem a bit mixed up, it's also becoming more accepting of people who are different. This is partly because everyone is connected through phones and the internet so ideas travel faster and we have access to more points of view.

Teens Make Language Fun: You know how your older sister or brother talks in a way you don't always get? Well, that's teenagers making language more fun and interesting for everyone. Eventually, these strange new words become common, and so the whole language evolves. It would be dull if everything always stayed the same, right?

City Changes Unites People: Sometimes, when neighbourhoods get fancier (known as gentrification), it can be a problem for the local people who already live there, as they may not be able to afford to live near their family and friends anymore. But, it can make things better for the people who already live there too. It also helps mix up neighbourhoods where everyone used to look the same, bringing different cultures together.

Nature Recovers After a Mess: Big disasters like earthquakes or floods might look terrible at first, but over time, they can help nature become stronger as the creatures and plants that survive are the best at adapting to hard conditions. So next time things get tough, the natural world is better prepared to deal with it.

Phones Keep Teens Busy: Teens today are always on their phones. Teachers and parents might complain, but that's not all bad. It keeps them from getting bored and maybe doing troublesome things like breaking stuff or graffiti.

Extinction Gives Others a Chance: It's tragic when animals or plants disappear forever, but it opens up a space for other ones to thrive.

ON THE UP

People Are Living Longer: Back when factories and steam engines were big, folks in Europe didn't usually make it past 35 years. But don't picture everyone dropping like flies in their 30s! Most of that was because many babies didn't make it, and there were diseases like smallpox and the plague. Nowadays, in rich countries, medicine and safety keep us alive.

230

Global Income Gap Is Shrinking: Even though some rich folks are getting richer, the gap between rich and poor countries is getting smaller. That's mostly because countries like China and India are improving living standards for millions. About half of the world's people now have a pretty good life, which is a big change from the past.

Fewer Kids Are Dying: Over 100 years ago, even in places like the US and UK, more than 10% of kids didn't make it past childhood. But thanks to doctors and safer stuff, hardly any kids in rich countries pass away early these days. More good news? In countries like India and Brazil, fewer kids are dying now than in rich countries back then!

People Are Having Fewer Babies: Some folks worry the world will get too crowded, but guess what? People around the world are having fewer babies. They think the global population will settle at around 11 billion by the end of the century. Places like Brazil, China, and parts of Africa already have fewer kids. It took richer countries a long time to do this, but these places managed it way faster.

Economies Are Growing Faster: The tech-savvy leaders like the US and Europe have been getting richer at a steady rate – about 2% more every year for 150 years. That means our money doubles about every 36 years. Sure, there were some tough times like the Great Depression, but overall, we're doing pretty well. Countries like China and India are catching up fast, growing at 10%, which means their money doubles every seven years.

Democracy Is Spreading: A long time ago, most people had to deal with rulers who didn't listen to them. But now, about half of the world's people live in democracies where they get a say in how things work. Some places are still not very democratic, but the optimists hope that this will change as they grow richer.

Conflict Levels Are Going Down: The world used to have lots of fights and big wars, especially in the past 500 years. But since the last big war, things have been way calmer, especially in Western Europe. They haven't had a war for three generations thanks to groups like the EU and the UN that try to keep peace. Gold star for behaviour!

RIDDLE ANSWERS!

Page 4: Trivia

Page 82: Language

AROUND THE WORLD IN 195 FACTS

Robin Why

FREE EBOOK

JOURNEY THE GLOBE FROM YOUR FAVOURITE ARMCHAIR

CLICK TO JOIN
my readers & get your FREE EBOOK

DISCOUNTS
BONUS TRIVIA
NEW BOOKS

SIGN UP AT WWW.ROBINWHY.COM

YOUR REVIEW MATTERS

I'm immensely grateful for your support in choosing this book! If you enjoyed the read, could you please take a moment to leave a review on Amazon? Your feedback is vital, especially for first-time and self-published authors, helping me to reach more readers and continue creating books you love. Thank you for being part of my literary journey!

Type in your link below to be taken straight to my Amazon review page...

US	robinwhy.com/wow**us**
UK	robinwhy.com/wow**uk**
Australia	robinwhy.com/wow**au**
Canada	robinwhy.com/wow**ca**

I'm excited to read your thoughts!

ABOUT THE AUTHOR

Hello, nice to meet you. I'm Robin Why. I navigate the skies to the far corners of this planet, gathering facts to build my towering nest of trivia.

With a beak for prose, I have become a sensation in both literary and ornithological circles, often found perched on typewriters and tweeting literary masterpieces in 280 characters or less.

When not writing, I enjoy flapping through incredible landscapes, seeking inspiration in the clouds, and squawking philosophical questions to unsuspecting worms.

My obsession with facts took flight when I discovered just how peculiar humans are. They never fail to amaze me.

So, dear trivia-lovers, I welcome you to nestle down for an excellent read. I'm here to take your mind on a migration like no other.

WWW.ROBINWHY.COM

Printed in Great Britain
by Amazon

60529423R00137